LOUIS ANDRIESSEN: *DE STAAT*

for Jayne

Louis Andriessen: *De Staat*

ROBERT ADLINGTON

University of Nottingham, UK

Published by
Ashgate Publishing Limited
Gower House
Croft Road
Aldershot
Hants GU11 3HR
England

Ashgate Publishing Company
Suite 420
101 Cherry Street
Burlington, VT 05401-4405
USA

Ashgate website: http://www.ashgate.com

British Library Cataloguing in Publication Data
Adlington, Robert
    Louis Andriessen : De Staat. – (Landmarks in music since 1950)
    1. Andriessen, Louis, 1939–. Staat
    I. Title
    780.9'2

Library of Congress Cataloging-in-Publication Data
Adlington, Robert.
    Louis Andriessen, De staat / Robert Adlington.
      p. cm. – (Landmarks in music since 1950)
    Includes bibliographical references and index.
    ISBN 0-7546-0925-1 (alk. paper)
      1. Andriessen, Louis, 1939– Staat. I. Title. II. Series.

    ML410.A6326A35 2004
    782.4'8–dc22

2003059519

ISBN 0 7546 0925 1

Typeset by Express Typesetters Ltd, Farnham
Printed and bound in Great Britain by TJ International Ltd, Padstow, Cornwall

Contents

List of Tables and Music Examples

Tables

Music Examples

General Editor's Preface

Apart from a few notable exceptions, specialist books on individual works composed since the end of the Second World War are thin on the ground. Detailed commentaries have been limited to necessarily less ambitious opera, concert and record booklets or published in journals, ranging from the overtly popular to the academically erudite. This new series of volumes devoted to contextual and analytical studies of single significant compositions (or coherent groups of works) aims to redress this balance by bringing together something of the excitement and immediacy of a concert-guide – in each case, a CD of the work itself is included with the book – with the insights of distinguished authors whose research areas provide the resources for windows of exploration into the circumstances surrounding the composition of the chosen work, its musical language and structure, its place in the composer's oeuvre, and its reception history. Additionally, the socio-political context of each composer and composition is illuminated by a selection of documents such as interviews, concert reviews, letters or diary extracts.

In deciding which works to choose, the publishers have been guided by a number of principles. It goes without saying that the composers themselves should command general respect (although popularity is not in itself a criterion of selection); the works should have been widely disseminated (although in certain cases – operas particularly – this is less important than positive critical evaluation and the availability of adequate recordings); a wide range of styles and aesthetics should be explored; and the selection of works should be international. The series is not an attempt to construct a canon of modern 'masterworks' – indeed its title is a self-definition of an intention to identify key works in the development of varied musical idioms and techniques since the death of Schoenberg. Inevitably, some compositions may be better known to the reader than others but all will provide opportunities to revisit (or discover) important landmarks on the constantly evolving map of modern music – to engage with a blend of scholarly analysis and colourful critical appraisal and to be better prepared for further excursions into music of the present day.

Robert Adlington's fascinating study of Andriessen's *De Staat* ('The Republic') sets the work in the turbulent world of Dutch music during the second half of the twentieth century and traces the composer's progression from his participation in contemporary reactions against the traditional dominance of the symphony orchestra to his current position as the most distinguished member of the Dutch musical establishment. Through a series of well-focused essays and analyses, *De Staat* is revealed as a consummate fusion of varied musical practices and ideologies – a challenging testimony to the breadth of Andriessen's musical sympathies and intellectual curiosity – and a landmark in personal, national and international terms. Thanks to the generosity of the publishers, it has been possible to include two of Andriessen's earlier works (one previously unavailable) on the CD which accompanies this book. It is particularly appropriate that this volume and these recordings should contribute to the celebration of the composer's 65th birthday (in 2004) and to the ongoing evaluation of his creative output.

Wyndham Thomas
University of Bristol

Acknowledgements

I have been the beneficiary of outstandingly generous assistance from many people whilst writing this book. First of all, I must thank Louis Andriessen for his warm support and encouragement for the project from the start, and for the stimulating and informative feedback he offered on drafts of each chapter. There will remain things in this book with which he disagrees, but I have always attempted to indicate where we diverge, and how. He knows that my sole intention has been to do justice to his wonderful music. Mirjam Zegers at Muziekgroep Nederland (the parent company of Andriessen's first publisher Donemus) has been a tireless and friendly intermediary in my communications with the composer, and she also provided me with some rare materials copied from Andriessen's archives.

I am indebted to my editor Wyndham Thomas for agreeing to include this book in his series, and for his sound advice and flexibility at every stage. At Ashgate, Rachel Lynch was particularly patient and accommodating in pursuing my ideas for the compact disc accompanying this book; I thank her for making them a reality, and for her efficiency and kindness in all our dealings. My copy-editor Bonnie Blackburn smoothed out many rough edges and helped me clarify my argument in a number of places.

A number of friends and colleagues somehow found time in their busy lives to read draft chapters and provide valuable feedback. Yayoi Uno Everett, who is currently writing a major study of Andriessen's music, has been a particularly generous collaborator, freely offering ideas, materials and friendship. My other readers were Jayne Carroll, Daniel Grimley, Tom Hall, Sam Hayden, Steen Kaargaard Nielsen, Philip Rupprecht, Elmer Schönberger and Pwyll ap Siôn. I hope they will recognize how much they have contributed to this book; for those places where I foolishly ignored their advice I apologize both to them and to the reader.

Many other people have offered invaluable ideas and assistance, of all kinds: Anne Allcock; David Allenby and Muireann Smyth at Boosey and Hawkes; Richard Baker; Linda van den Beld at the Dutch Ministry of Education, Culture and Science; Ger van den Beuken at the Muziekgroep Nederland archive; Barbara Bleij; Joël Bons; Henk Borgdorff; Gerard Broers at the Gaudeamus Foundation Library; Mervyn Cooke; Jonathan Cross; Lynn

Fotheringham; Sarah Holmes at the London Sinfonietta; Jacqueline Kelderman at the Asko and Schönberg Ensembles; James Kennedy; Geert van Keulen; Manuela Lageweg and Sander van Maas at the Netherlands Wind Ensemble; Gillian Moore; Keith Potter; Elmer Schönberger; Michiel Schuijer; Catherine Sutton; Graham Taylor; Peter Wright; Kristen Thorner; and Steve Richards.

Diana van Gent undertook some of the more arduous translation work involved in this project, and cheerfully checked many of my own translations. All responsibility for misreadings and infelicities lies of course with me.

I was fortunate to have a year's research leave in which to write this book. My protracted absence from teaching has certainly added to the burden carried by my colleagues in the Music Department at the University of Nottingham, and I thank them for their forbearance and support. One semester of my leave was funded by an Arts and Humanities Research Board grant. David Clarke and Arnold Whittall generously agreed to support my application to the AHRB, and Peter Elford at the University of Nottingham skilfully guided me through the application process. Some of my travel and translation expenses were met by a grant from the New Lecturers Fund of the University of Nottingham Research Support Office, with matching funding from the University's School of Humanities.

Music examples from *De Staat* are © Copyright 1994 by Boosey & Hawkes Music Publishers Ltd, while those from *Hymne to the Memory of Darius Milhaud* are © Copyright 1978 by Donemus (controlled by BHMP for the UK, British Commonwealth, Eire and the Western Hemisphere). Reproduced by permission of Boosey & Hawkes Music Publishers Ltd.

Note on References

I have followed Dutch convention in my references to names. The particles common in Dutch names ('Van der', 'De', 'Op de', etc.) are appended for individual references to surnames alone in the main text, but the alphabetical listing in the Bibliography is according to last name without prefix. Thus 'Van Akkeren 1977' is listed in the Bibliography as 'Akkeren, Arnold van (1977)'.

Introduction

As this book was being sent to press, a new advertising campaign for Heineken beer appeared on British television. The advert sought to confirm the centrality of Heineken to Dutch life by conducting what it called the 'Dutch Tolerance Test'. It shows a supermarket somewhere in the Netherlands, populated solely by shoppers visibly pursuing various 'alternative' lifestyles: roller-blading bondage fetishists; newly-wed male couples; body-pierced hippies. The peace is disturbed, however, when a young man timidly enquires, to the disapproving looks of all around him, if they sell any other beer than Heineken: he is summarily ejected from the shop (by a nose-ringed security guard) as a 'weirdo'. The caricature is crude and (in keeping with most British beer commercials) mildly offensive, but it is nevertheless representative of a common perception of Dutch culture. During the 1960s and 1970s the Netherlands became a byword for social progressiveness and the permissive society, a reputation it has retained to this day. From being widely viewed in the 1950s as 'a quaint, "old-fashioned" society, steeped in the traditions and conventions of a previous age' (Kennedy 1995, p. 4), the Netherlands transformed itself, with relatively little violent conflict and (eventually) the cooperation of governing authorities and establishment institutions, into the most apparently forward-looking of societies. The impact made by the anti-Islamic, anti-immigrant politician Pim Fortuyn during his brief career in 2002 – an impact felt both in the Netherlands and overseas – was a measure of the extent to which the country's very identity was being thrown into question.[1]

Louis Andriessen's *De Staat* ('The Republic') (1976), with its exuberance, strength of conviction and noisy lack of refinement, epitomizes this image of the Netherlands. It quickly came to be viewed as the 'standard-bearer for contemporary Dutch music',[2] and its impact on other composers, both within the Netherlands and beyond, was to be significant and long

---

[1] Fortuyn gained considerable popular support in the campaign for the 2002 general election, but was assassinated nine days before the polls.

[2] Frits van der Waa, review of the premiere of the two-piano version of *De Staat*, *De Volkskrant*, 17 November 1984, p. 11.

lasting.[3] It was also a breakthrough piece for the composer, constituting, in its extended scale, pop-influenced orchestration and preoccupation with philosophical topics, 'the work in which Andriessen reached full maturity' (Van der Waa 2000, p. 14). As winner of the 1977 UNESCO International Rostrum of Composers prize and through widely distributed recordings it led in no small part to the international reputation that Andriessen enjoys today, both as a composer of large-scale concert and theatre works, and as a composition teacher. If *De Staat* thus marks a 'beginning', it also bears witness to the milieu of protest and activism from which it sprang. There has been a tendency, particularly in Britain and the United States where Andriessen's earlier music is little known, to view *De Staat* solely in the context of the larger works that follow. There are certain respects, though, in which it can be seen as a summatory statement, even marking the *end* of an era for its composer – particularly the four years Andriessen spent performing with the Orkest De Volharding (1972 to 1976), which coincided precisely with its gestation and composition. During this period, his music was explicitly aimed at reflecting the circumstances of its performance, which in the case of De Volharding were frequently far removed from the 'official' mainstream of concert hall and symphony orchestra.

This book proceeds on the basis that *De Staat*, likewise, is not properly understood by approaching it as an autonomous, self-standing artwork, and that a full grasp of the ideological and musical context from which it sprang is essential if it is to make its fullest impact. In Chapter 1 I give an account of Andriessen's involvement in the protests and struggle for cultural renewal that characterized the Netherlands in the sixties and seventies. Few prominent contemporary composers have played as significant a role as political activist and agitator for cultural change, but while this aspect of Andriessen's career is the stuff of legend in the Netherlands, the detail is little known overseas. Andriessen's political commitment is made particularly intriguing given his background in rather inaccessible forms of musical modernism: I begin Chapter 1 by tracing the tortuous negotiations with avant-gardism undertaken by his early music as his political outlook gained focus.

Chapter 2 examines three important influences on Andriessen's musical idiom as it evolved in the 1970s, and offers an opportunity for a more detailed assessment of the works leading up to *De Staat*, especially those written for the Orkest De Volharding. As such, it introduces some of the stylistic features

---

[3] Two early, prominent examples of this influence are the Dutch composer Otto Ketting's *Symphony for Saxophones and Orchestra* (1978) and John Adams's *Harmonium* (1980).

of *De Staat* that are subjected to greater scrutiny in Chapter 3. This chapter, in addition to giving an overview of the work's form, pays particular attention to the distinctive harmonic language of *De Staat* – one that hovers fascinatingly between the worlds of tonality and atonality, and that has proved one of the work's most influential features for younger composers. Chapter 4 moves to an assessment of *De Staat* in the light of Andriessen's musical and political preoccupations during the late sixties and early seventies. Here, the Plato text that Andriessen sets in *De Staat* assumes greater importance, as does his attitude to the work's performers and listeners, and the work's reception history. Finally, Chapter 5 is an interview with Andriessen in which he reflects on various aspects of *De Staat* from the perspective of more than a quarter of a century after its first performance.

The compact disc accompanying this book forms an integral part of my study. *De Staat* is represented by a 1978 live performance by the Netherlands Wind Ensemble and Lucas Vis, who had given the premiere two years earlier. This recording, which has never before been issued on compact disc, is impressive testament to the thriving 'ensemble culture' of which *De Staat* is, in many ways, a celebration. It also offers a somewhat fiercer account of the work than the later commercial recording by the Schönberg Ensemble and Reinbert de Leeuw.[4] Two earlier works are also included. *Il Principe* (1974), a little-known choral setting of texts by Machiavelli, anticipates a number of features of *De Staat*. No commercial recording exists, and so the opportunity to include this 1974 recording from the archive of the Dutch broadcaster NCRV here is particularly welcome. *De Volharding* (1972) is better known, for it is the piece that launched the Orkest De Volharding, and that also first unambiguously announced Andriessen's involvement with minimalism. The recording is taken from the work's rowdy premiere; it gives a good idea of both the inimitable sound of the Orkest De Volharding, and the lively musical culture of which it was a part. References are made to the compact disc at various stages in my text. A number of the figures and examples in Chapter 3 include precise timings to help identification of passages on the recording of *De Staat*. Appendix B also details the timing of significant moments in the score, and can be used as an aid for other parts of my text.

---

[4] Reinbert de Leeuw's 1990 recording is on Elektra Nonesuch 7559-79251-2.

Chapter 1

Music and Politics: Early Works, Protest and the Orkest De Volharding

At the beginning of my interview with Louis Andriessen (see Ch. 5) he declares: 'For me *De Staat* is a kind of extension of De Volharding.' The assertion of the connection between *De Staat* and Andriessen's activities in the years leading up to it grounds the discussion in this chapter. Rather than springing from nowhere – the impression sometimes given by representations of his oeuvre – *De Staat* is rooted in the concerns and preoccupations of the late sixties and early seventies. Andriessen's involvement with the Orkest De Volharding ('Perseverance Orchestra'), a 'street ensemble' made up of jazz and classical musicians with an avowedly political mission, coincides precisely with the gestation and composition of *De Staat*. An account of the founding and ideology of De Volharding thus forms the final part of this chapter, in the belief that its importance for *De Staat* has not generally been fully appreciated. De Volharding was, in turn, the outcome of a period of noisy protest against existing structures for the performance of new music: during the latter half of the 1960s Andriessen developed an understanding of the relation of music and politics that was to remain a matter of firm conviction thereafter. The wider culture of protest in the Netherlands to which he belonged has its own colourful appeal, and it forms a backdrop to my account, in the central part of this chapter, of his activities during this time. Even before a politicized outlook manifested itself, however, Andriessen's music evinced a discomfort with compositional orthodoxies. As the first section of this chapter is intended to show, the open indebtedness of *De Staat* to other musics, which receives further attention later in this book, reflects a long-established interest in evading singular stylistic affiliations.

Beginnings

Andriessen's reputation is that of an iconoclast, someone keen to distance himself from musical tradition and the musical establishment. Yet there is no living composer more indebted to the musically privileged circumstances of his youth, and Andriessen has always acknowledged the fact. Andriessen's father Hendrik was a giant of modern Dutch music: composer, organist, author and (at various times) director of the Utrecht and Hague Conservatories.[1] Hendrik's Catholicism contributed to a leaning towards Latinate and especially French culture, and this interest left Louis with an abiding love of French Romantic music – and an antipathy towards German musical tradition (Trochimczyk (ed.) 2002, pp. 9, 175). Louis's older brother Jurriaan was also a formative figure. In the mid-fifties he travelled to the United States, and returned with a stash of jazz records that were greedily consumed by the young Louis. Complementing these familial influences was the composer Kees van Baaren, with whom Louis took lessons at the Hague Conservatory from 1956. Van Baaren was one of the first Dutch composers to have a thorough grasp of the revolutionary compositional techniques of the Second Viennese School, and Andriessen was soon experimenting confidently with serialism. His first published work, *Séries* for two pianos (1958), was one of the first strict serial compositions by a Dutch composer.[2] Its twelve short movements predictably show the influence of Boulez's *Structures*, but much independence too: No. 7, for instance, commits the solecism of dwelling throughout on a sustained A minor triad.

Andriessen's interest in serialism was quickly counterbalanced by a fascination with the alternative avant-garde of John Cage. Another recent Van Baaren recruit, Misha Mengelberg, returned from the 1958 Darmstadt Summer School 'with all these stories of Cage doing crazy lectures, and we were very excited. We started reading koans, studying Zen Buddhism at that time. We were 18!' (Andriessen, in Whitehead 1999, p. 15). Like Andriessen, Mengelberg had grown up listening to and playing both twentieth-century classical music and jazz. The two were soon swapping letters on a daily basis, and in 1962 they collaborated with the artist Willem de Ridder and a number of other composers to form the Mood Engineering Society, a collective dedicated to various kinds of post-Cagian conceptual performance (Schouten 1973, p. 58). De Ridder and Mengelberg later pursued this interest in performance art as participants at the Fluxus festivals in Amsterdam and Rotterdam in 1963 and 1964 (Van der Klis (ed.) 2000, p. 256; Kellein 1995, p. 17).

---

[1] For fuller details of Andriessen's early life, see Trochimczyk (ed.) 2002 and Andriessen 2002.

[2] Andriessen was pipped to the post by Ton de Leeuw, whose First String Quartet (1958) is recognized as the first fully serial composition by a Dutch composer; see Peters 1995, p. 48.

Andriessen's own music from the late fifties and early sixties reflects the diversity of his musical interests – and in so doing, it set the pattern for his entire career. *Séries* was followed in 1959 by *Nocturnen* for soprano and chamber orchestra, in which serial organization is almost completely absent and homage is paid instead to the sumptuous orchestration and harmonic staticity of earlier twentieth-century French music. Four works from 1961 explore quite different territory again: *Ittrospezione* for piano duet and *Paintings* for recorder and piano are graphic scores (the first full of visual jokes, the second more earnest); *Aanloop en sprongen* ('Run up and jump') for flute, oboe and clarinet and *Trois Pièces* for piano left hand present a fluent, relaxed neoclassicism that is a world away from such conceits and experimentation.

Despite Andriessen's lack of dogmatism on questions of style and technique he remained sufficiently interested in the serial avant-garde to visit Darmstadt in 1963,[3] and following the completion of his studies at the Hague Conservatory the next step was clear: 'The question was, "Do I go to Boulez, or to Stockhausen, or to Berio?" That was the only choice one had when moving in that direction. There was no question of doing anything else at all' (Andriessen, in Trochimczyk (ed.) 2002, p. 15). Unsurprisingly, he chose Berio, whose music he found 'the most musical and the most "festive" ... Berio was just more fun and better to listen to' (in Koning and Jansen 1981, p. 14). He took lessons over a period of three years – firstly in Milan (1962–63) and then Berlin (1964–65). Andriessen later summed up the nature of his relationship with Berio:

> This is what I learned about from Luciano Berio: fish, Marxism, phonetics, open form, the emancipation of women, Joyce, André Masson, caviar, olive oil, fresh vegetables, to listen with acute attention and to be critical in the same way. And this is what I gave him in exchange: the transcription of the Azerbaijani song from a 78 record of Cathy Berberian, which was later used at the end of the *Folk Songs*; and more significantly in terms of the spirit of the 60s, I showed to Luciano the discs of a vocal ensemble then called Les Double Six, great French singers who later became the Swingle Singers for whom Berio wrote his *Sinfonia*.[4]

---

[3] Andriessen wrote a polite article on Darmstadt for the journal *De Gids*: see Andriessen 1963.

[4] From *Il Giornale della Musica online*, 164 (October 2000), <http://www.giornaledellamusica.it/cartaceo/articoli/2000/164/164_03.htm>, accessed 5 December 2002.

Berio's influence was clearly as much political and philosophical (not to mention culinary) as it was musical. Berio had recently completed the overtly political music-drama *Passaggio*, for instance, and Andriessen's political sensibilities were further honed by his experience of Berlin, whose post-Wall tensions he hated (Trochimczyk (ed.) 2002, p. 17). Musically, Andriessen's later compositional interest in unison melody, slow harmonic rhythm and punchy orchestration can all perhaps be traced back to Berio. In later chapters we will see that there are particular points of connection between Berio's music and *De Staat*.

However, even during this period Andriessen was clearly not entirely comfortable toeing the avant-garde line. This is clear from a shorthand entry in his journal dating from May 1965 (reproduced in Andriessen 1968c). In it, he recalls the fatigue incurred by copying the intricate score of his formidable orchestral piece *Ittrospezione II* (1963) – a kind of 'despair' over the work's complexity, which seemed 'absurd after [Boulez's] *Structures* and the three Sonatas. Slavework, unnecessary.... After this, I felt that composition had to be abolished' (ibid., p. 8). He found relief in 'wild piano improvisations', which he later set down in the graphic score of *Registers* for piano (1963). In fact, Andriessen did eventually return to 'composition', writing *Ittrospezione III* (1964–65) as an exercise for Berio. But this latest work reflected the abhorrence of exactitude expressed in his journal – principally through a wholehearted embracing of the concept of 'mobile form' developed by the American composer and pioneer of graphic scores Earle Brown. Andriessen had heard Brown's *Available Forms I* for orchestra (1961) at a concert in The Hague (Andriessen 1995b, p. 110); in this piece, musical events arranged on several unbound pages may be combined in different ways at the whim of the conductor. *Ittrospezione III* enacts roughly the same idea: blocks of contrasting material are crudely juxtaposed and superimposed in a largely random manner. To demonstrate the non-definitive nature of the piece, Andriessen wrote several different versions for differing ensembles. In theory, the musical materials of this 'open collage'[5] could be endlessly rearranged.

Ittrospezione III marked an end-point, rather than a way forward. On concluding his studies with Berio, Andriessen made a symbolic declaration of independence with a series of pieces that defiantly refused to align themselves with any one stylistic tendency. The first of these, *Souvenirs d'enfance* (1966), a collection of pieces for amateur pianist, signalled a return to some of the musical preoccupations of his youth. It contains a 'Rondo' dating from 1954,

---

[5] Ernst Vermeulen, review of 1971 Holland Festival, *Sonorum Speculum*, **46** (Spring 1971), 4.

a 'Nocturne' written in the style of Fauré, and a serial 'Etude pour les timbres' written for Andriessen's final exam at the Hague Conservatory. Additionally, there are a number of parody pieces in contrasting twentieth-century styles, ranging from an octatonic 'Sonatensatz' – included, as the preface declares, as 'an example of How Not To Compose'[6] – to a graphically notated piece called 'Blokken'. Despite the light-hearted impression made by the collection, there was a serious underlying aesthetic motivation, clearly expressed in an article that Andriessen wrote a couple of years later: *Souvenirs* sought to 'make all areas of music contemporary' (Andriessen 1968d, p. 179).

The idea that one might combine within a work a variety of different styles, both old and new, was much abroad in the late 1960s. Berio himself was to write perhaps the most famous example in the third movement (written in 1968) of his *Sinfonia*, and the same year saw the composition of Schnittke's Second Violin Sonata and Pärt's Credo. But these famous examples were preceded by 'quotation' and 'collage' pieces from George Rochberg, Bernd Alois Zimmermann and Henri Pousseur, amongst others. Andriessen, too, anticipated Berio and Schnittke with his *Anachronie I* for orchestra (1967), a witty patchwork of parodied musical styles which includes quotations from Brahms, Roussel, Franck, and Jurriaan and Hendrik Andriessen.[7] 'Collage' and 'quotation' works of this kind were of course partly a reaction to the emphasis placed on originality and stylistic purity by the fifties' avant-garde. Particularly important, for Andriessen, was the possibility of mixing 'high' and 'low' musics: *Anachronie I* delights in pitting pop songs, big-band jazz and clichéd film music against more 'elevated' compositional styles. In discussing the piece, Andriessen referred to parallel developments in the visual arts: 'Just as pop art reflects reality, often with the help of magnifying glasses and distorting mirrors, so *Anachronie I* is a reflection of musical reality' (Andriessen 1968d, p. 179).

But looming largest for Andriessen at this time, as for many other composers, was the example set at the beginning of the twentieth century by the dedicatee of *Anachronie I*, Charles Ives. For Andriessen, 'the growing importance of Ives's music in Holland was directly connected to the democratic movement there' (Andriessen, in Peters 1994, p. 616). The Provo actions had just begun in Amsterdam (these are described in the next section of this chapter), and the music's lack of decorum and inclusiveness with regard

---

[6] Andriessen later described the piece as being in the style of Henk Badings (Andriessen 1968d, p. 178).

[7] A comprehensive list of *Anachronie I*'s quotations and style-references is given in Desmedt 1988, pp. 130–32.

to musical style seemed completely in tune with the times. Andriessen also detected a certain kinship with Stravinsky, whose music he was increasingly evoking in his own works, as well as mentioning in hallowed terms in the essays he wrote for the literary journal *De Gids* during this period.[8] Ives, like Stravinsky, was 'one of the few composers who found music more interesting than himself' (Andriessen 1968d, p. 179). His stylistic pluralism implied a certain 'depersonification', which could be compared to the cool objectivity of Stravinsky's classicism even though it sounded nothing like it. The idea that music should be 'about music', rather than about the composer, has remained central to Andriessen's aesthetic outlook ever since.[9]

Anachronie I ends disconcertingly with what Andriessen called 'typical sixties Darmstadt music, entirely petrified [*versteend*]' (in Koning and Jansen 1981, p. 14). He later interpreted this as signalling a 'personal farewell to Darmstadt' (Van Rossum and Smit 1994, p. 11). But his next piece showed that his involvement with the serial avant-garde, rather than being a thing of the past, was now simply one stylistic option amongst many. *Contra Tempus* for large ensemble (1968), with its twelve-note row, carefully calculated proportional scheme and exploration of the interplay of harmonic and melodic function is fundamentally an uncompromising exercise in avant-garde compositional technique.[10] Elmer Schönberger has suggested that *Contra Tempus* lays down 'elements of a blueprint for the larger pieces of the seventies' (Schönberger 1993, p. 215). Its orchestration (brass and keyboards, reduced winds and strings), severe block form (inspired by Stravinsky amongst others) and exploration of static musical processes certainly anticipate *De Staat*. Andriessen's other works since 1966 may have insisted that stylistic pluralism should be part of this future compositional agenda, but, as *Contra Tempus* makes clear, it was to be a pluralism that accommodated conceptual adventurousness, ambitious design, and a challenging and provocative harmonic language.

Revolution

In a reminiscence of his first encounter with fellow Van Baaren student Reinbert de Leeuw at the Hague Conservatory, Louis Andriessen recalls sitting in the Conservatory canteen: 'Through the disconsolate neon-lighting and the

---

[8] See, for instance, Andriessen 1968a and Andriessen 1968b.

[9] Andriessen's 'classicism' is discussed in greater depth in Ch. 2.

[10] Andriessen discusses the piece in Andriessen 1968d.

faded brown colour of the warped plywood shelves, the fifties hung around you like a heavy mist' (Andriessen 1995b, p. 108). A sense of frustration with, even contempt for, the stultifying conservatism of Dutch bourgeois society was already common amongst young intellectuals in the fifties. The generation of writers who had grown up during the war were amongst the first to express this frustration openly. The novels of Willem Frederik Hermans, Gerard Kornelis van het Reve and Harry Mulisch reflected critically on the quiescence of much of the Dutch establishment in the face of the German occupation during the Second World War, and on the provincialism and parochialism of Dutch society. Their writing was characterized by both anti-establishmentarianism and a feeling that existence was fundamentally futile and senseless (Meijer 1971).

It was not until the start of the sixties, however, that this discontent crystallized into a protest movement with concrete political goals, one that was ultimately to achieve a great measure of success. The basis for this movement was an unlikely confluence of disaffected youth, performance art, and a few eccentric and persistent individuals, which created a focus for growing public unrest about issues such as the nuclear threat and the Vietnam War. Robert Jasper Grootveld, a former window cleaner and experimental artist, was a key figure. In 1962 Grootveld returned to the Netherlands from a trip to Africa convinced that industrialized society was being poisoned by the products of greedy corporations, particularly tobacco. Dressing in costume and styling himself the 'Anti-Smoke Sorcerer' and 'Medicine Man of the Western Asphalt Jungle' (Shetter 1987, p. 236), he held regular theatrical 'happenings' against consumer society in the centre of Amsterdam, first in a rented garage and then in Spui square. A form of artistic expression that had hitherto been the preserve of avant-garde galleries and university campuses thus found itself transformed into democratized street theatre, conveying a strong political message that appealed to drifting teenagers and the arty intelligentsia alike.

It was at one of these happenings in May 1965 that Roel van Duyn, a philosophy student at the University of Amsterdam, distributed leaflets announcing the birth of the Provo movement (Voeten 1990).[11] The Provos (derived from *provocateurs*) were a loose alliance of young activists, eager to harness the social discontent expressed at Grootveld's performances to more concrete revolutionary goals. With Grootveld's cooperation, the Provos began to coordinate the happenings. Influenced in part by the surrealist painter and Situationist Constant Nieuwenhuys, who during the early sixties developed a vision of 'a play-filled culture', the Provos 'sought to make Amsterdam a

---

[11] My account of the Provos is indebted to Voeten's excellent article.

"ludiek centrum" of individual freedom' (Kennedy 1995, pp. 1–3, 244). Their gatherings and publications combined seriousness and playfulness in equal measure, a characteristic that was to be replicated in later protests against musical institutions, and which may also be heard in much Dutch music during the sixties and seventies – Andriessen's included. Unfortunately, as growing public disquiet over Vietnam swelled interest in the happenings, they also took on a more confrontational character: arrests and scuffles with the police were common during 1965. The most serious violence occurred during the wedding procession of Princess Beatrix and the German Prince Claus in March 1966, when smoke bombs thrown by the Provos sparked an aggressive police response. Further violent disturbances ensued over the next few months.

The overtly creative element of Provo, and its connections with avant-garde performance art, helped speed the politicization of artistic communities in Amsterdam and other Dutch cities. In the late sixties, the activities of the Provos were counterpointed by a number of protests directed towards established institutions in the arts world. In music, five of Van Baaren's students – Andriessen, Mengelberg, De Leeuw, Peter Schat and Jan van Vlijmen – took a particularly prominent role, and ultimately 'the Five' (as they became known) would be credited with nothing less than 'shaking Dutch musical life out of its suffocating provincialism' (Krook 1976). Their principal target was the symphony orchestra, which had held a privileged position in Dutch musical life since before the Second World War, when orchestral music had been the only art form to receive central governmental subsidy on account of its apparent autonomy from potentially corrupting social meaning (MINOCW 1998). In particular the Five focused on the most prominent symbol of the Dutch musical establishment, the Amsterdam Concertgebouw Orchestra. Initially their campaign concerned the simple matter of programming policy. In an open letter published in the *Algemeen Handelsblad* five days after the disrupted royal wedding, the Five argued that the existing artistic direction of the Concertgebouw Orchestra was 'incompetent' with regard to contemporary music, and proposed that the avant-garde composer Bruno Maderna should be installed as principal conductor alongside Bernard Haitink.[12] Maderna's concerts with The Hague's Residentie Orkest had featured distinctive combinations of old and new music, which at least in part overcame the ghettoizing tendency of the Concertgebouw Orchestra's occasional short series of *actuele muziek* (contemporary music) concerts. A number of meetings between the Five and the orchestra yielded no further

---

[12] For more details on this campaign see Jansen 1980.

progress,[13] and so the composers decided to organize a public debate, under the auspices of *De Gids* (Samama 2001, p. 747). The composers received expressions of support from an impressive range of musicians, artists and other eminent figures in the arts (see Samama 1986, p. 260), and, partly with the assistance of some lively press debate in the weeks that followed, their cause was catapulted into the public gaze.

A pamphlet later compiled by the Five about the affair, *Achter de muziek aan* ('Following the music'), stated that 'In the first place we ask nothing more than that the Concertgebouw Orchestra live up to its image as a stimulus in European musical life' (cited in Koopmans 1976b, p. 23). If the Concert-gebouw had failed in this respect, in other areas of Dutch musical life this was an exciting time. New ensembles and institutions were springing up to cater for the demands of creative musicians of all kinds. 1966 saw both the founding of a new chamber orchestra dedicated to the performance of challenging new music (the Amsterdams Studenten Kamer Orkest – later to become the Asko Ensemble), and the reorganization of the Netherlands Wind Ensemble under the conductor Edo de Waart, in which guise it was to become heavily involved in contemporary music. An energetic early music movement was gathering momentum in Amsterdam around the figures of Gustav Leonhardt and Frans Brüggen, providing further fuel for the campaign against traditional symphony orchestras. The field of improvisation attained a new level of institutional stability and renown with the founding, in 1967, of the Instant Composers Pool by Misha Mengelberg and the jazz musicians Willem Breuker and Han Bennink. And the following year saw the founding of the Studio for Electro-Instrumental Music (or STEIM), a resource for composers and improvisers wishing to work with live electronic music (Koopmans 1976b, p. 22). If orchestras were not going to change, then new outlets were needed for the creative preoccupations of contemporary musicians.

One of the most widely publicized events to occur in the wake of these developments was the extravagantly titled *Politiek-demonstratief experimen-teel* ('political-activist experimental') concert held at the Carré Theatre in Amsterdam on 30 May 1968.[14] From its inception, this concert of music by Andriessen, Mengelberg and Schat was intended as a riposte to established concert life. Instead of the Concertgebouw or another dedicated classical concert hall, the promoters chose the Carré Theatre, an old circus hall allegedly destined for demolition (Mineur 1989, p. 19). The event thus became

---

[13] Details of these meetings are given in Royen 1989.

[14] Following the Amsterdam performance, the concert toured to Rotterdam, The Hague and Eindhoven.

a statement of resistance against both the rarefied environment in which composed music is typically consumed, and the spirit of commercial speculation that was widely perceived to be endangering Amsterdam's cultural and architectural heritage. And in place of a standard orchestra, a 'mobiel ensemble' was assembled with musicians drawn from six different orchestras (although the core was provided by the Netherlands Wind Ensemble and the Percussion Group Amsterdam). The idea that professional musicians should be able to move freely between ensembles and choose which music they play, soon to become a key principle for Andriessen, had its first trial run here.

However, two events led to the 'PDE' concert acquiring dramatic extra-political significance. Earlier in 1968, Peter Schat travelled to Castro's Cuba, and returned full of revolutionary political zeal. It was at this stage that the concert became more explicitly directed towards 'the undermining of capitalism' (see Samama 1986, p. 260), an intention baldly announced by the programme book which juxtaposed articles by the composers with quotations from Mao, Guevara, Trotsky, Adorno and Marcuse. No one could have predicted, however, that the concert would also turn out to coincide with the most iconic manifestation of all sixties' protest, the strikes and revolts in Paris of May 1968.[15] These had climaxed in the week prior to the PDE concert, when up to 10 million workers throughout France joined a general strike. De Gaulle himself had temporarily disappeared on 29 May, sparking fears of a communist takeover; on the day of the concert Dutch newspapers carried dramatic headlines declaring 'Paris in confusion'.[16] By this time, the focus of the Paris protest had spread from the Sorbonne to the nearby national theatre, the Odéon. The Dutch authorities, already unnerved by student protests throughout the Netherlands, were afraid that a similarly inflammatory situation might develop at Carré. Around 200 police surrounded the theatre on the night of the concert, ready for anything (Samama 1986, p. 261).

In the event, and in spite of ardent political speeches between the pieces and the red flags and posters of Castro and Guevara draped around the walls of the auditorium, there was no uprising: in the words of Han G. Hoekstra, 'music was made, but not history' (Hoekstra 1968). Indeed there was some understandable bemusement at the apparent disparity between the overtly politicized trappings of the concert and the music itself.[17] The latter was hardly

---

[15] For an account of these events see Brown 1974.

[16] *De Telegraaf*, 30 May 1968, p. 1.

[17] See, for instance, the 'vox pop' reactions in Hoekstra 1968. Hoekstra's article is entitled 'Madurodam-revolutie in Carré': Madurodam is a miniature town amusement park in The Hague.

consonant with a popular revolution. Andriessen's *Contra Tempus*, despite its Machaut quotations, remains a tough, post-Darmstadt exercise in formal proportion and textural experimentation. Misha Mengelberg was represented by *Hello Windyboys*, the title of which – as well as mischievously waging its own guerilla action against the earnest 'politiek-demonstratief' element of the evening – refers to the work's two groups of wind instruments, which are placed in different spaces and communicate through a sound system.[18] (At Carré, a transparent, inflatable sound chamber was used for one of the groups.) Only Schat's contribution to the evening directly alluded to the wider political context: in its name, *On Escalation*; in its dedication, 'in memoriam Ernesto Che Guevara'; and in its musical procedures, which pitted conducted strings and winds against 'excluded' percussion, the latter gradually undermining the former until the 'dictator-conductor' is completely overthrown (Vermeulen 1989, p. 300).

If the PDE concert had a less than dramatic impact politically speaking, it nevertheless marked a shift from the essentially musical dispute of the Maderna campaign towards an awareness that problems in the musical sphere were bound up with broader political questions. The Five would soon be associated with a document that unambiguously declared: 'The official musical culture is not universal. It belongs to only one class, the bourgeoisie, which uses it to pursue ideological self-affirmation – to seek its own identity.'[19] Where the Concertgebouw Orchestra had initially been an enemy because of its failure to programme new music effectively, now it was targeted because of its association with the social elite and its use to promote Dutch trade with politically suspect regimes overseas (including, in the eyes of the protestors, the United States).[20] Musical production, in other words, was viewed as unavoidably implicated with the workings of society. The organization of musical life reflected the organization of society and worked to uphold its imbalances and injustices; those who sought social renewal could not remain complicit with the musical status quo.

On the other hand, there remained an insistence in the various pamphlets and communiqués associated with the Five that *music itself* is apolitical – for it is, to quote from the PDE concert programme (which in turn echoes Stravinsky), 'incapable of expressing anything at all, let alone of communicating political views'. Not only can music itself not change society, but it 'can't even evoke or nourish the growing disgust with late capitalism and all

---

[18] See Whitehead 1999, pp. 68–69 for a description of Mengelberg's piece.

[19] From a pamphlet issued in 1970; cited in Koopmans 1976b, p. 25.

[20] See 'The Nutcrackers Information Bulletin', cited in ibid., p. 23.

its economic and fascistic violence' (cited in Koopmans 1976b, p. 23). Thus, a leftist radicalism regarding the conditions of performance was combined with an insistence that musical styles should not be held culpable for the social meanings that get attached to them – a laissez-faire attitude that was closer to Stravinsky than Adorno. This stance was to remain central to Andriessen's own outlook in the seventies, as we will see.

Reconstructie ('Reconstruction'), the large music-theatre work on which the Five worked for a year following the PDE concert, was to bear out their continuing conviction that musical idioms cultivated by an intellectual minority could plausibly carry the message of popular revolution. Meanwhile, other fields in the arts were experiencing their own crises of conscience. In 1969 the Professional Association of Visual Artists (or BBK) organized the occupation of museums throughout the Netherlands, and the 'Action Group Tomato' embarked on a concerted campaign against the established repertory theatre (which involved the throwing of smoke bombs as well as tomatoes) (Kennedy 1995, p. 253; MINOCW 1998; Vermeulen 1994, p. 21). The disturbances soon spread to music. In October, students in the town of Tilburg disrupted a concert by the local Brabants Orchestra. This provided the trigger for what has since been called 'the constituting myth of Dutch musical life' (Peters 1994, p. 610) – the *Notenkraker* ('Nutcracker') protest of 17 November 1969.

The 'Nutcracker action group' included four of the Five (Jan van Vlijmen did not participate), as well as a number of other musicians and students.[21] Its name (invented by Harry Mulisch) combines two puns. In Dutch *noten* means 'musical notes' as well as 'nuts'; but more significantly, *krakers* are 'squatters', and squatting – and the lack of affordable housing – had become an increasingly contentious issue in Amsterdam towards the end of the 1960s (Shetter 1987, p. 241). On the evening of 17 November, members of the group scattered themselves amongst the audience at the Amsterdam Concertgebouw for a concert by the Concertgebouw Orchestra under Bernard Haitink. The protest began as soon as Haitink gave his first upbeat. Toy clickers, nutcrackers, rattles and tooters began to sound around the hall; leaflets declaring that the Orchestra was 'a status-symbol of the ruling elite in our society' and demanding a public discussion about the running of the orchestra were dropped from the balcony; and a BBK banner was unfurled.[22]

---

[21] See the list in Mineur 1989, p. 32. Her account is the most detailed source on the activities of the Nutcrackers.

[22] The leaflet is reproduced in Peters 1994, p. 615. Further useful sources on the protest include Giskes 1991; Samama 2001; Schouten 1973; Vermeulen 1989.

As Haitink stopped and left the platform, the real uproar began. Protestors mounted the stage to distribute leaflets amongst the musicians, and demands for a public discussion were shouted through a megaphone. The audience, meanwhile, set about silencing the protest, and a near-riot ensued. Musicians and stewards joined the fray, and the protestors were manhandled towards the exits. As Peter Schat recalled, only the arrival of the police prevented any further violence: 'I was almost murdered in the gangway, by members of the orchestra and the public. He did it! Him! They wanted to kill me with an iron table, genuinely.... The police rescued me' (in Schouten 1973, p. 63). After fifteen minutes, the concert was able to resume and continue uninterrupted.

The aggressive reaction of the concert-going public to the Nutcrackers' stunt might have been interpreted as a sign of the venom with which the 'ruling elite' was prepared to defend its interests. But the offence caused to the audience of 17 November is better explained by the fact that it was not a 'typical' Concertgebouw Orchestra audience at all. The evening had been organized by the Netherlands Theatre Centre as a subsidized 'popular concert' for people who were not subscribers or regular attenders at the Concertgebouw (De Beer 1994). If there was an 'elite' at the Nutcracker protest, therefore, it was arguably the protestors themselves. As a result, it was all too easy for their action to be portrayed as an infringement of personal freedom – as Walter Maas, the founder of the Gaudeamus Foundation for new music, implicitly did in comparing the protest to the techniques of the Nazis (Peters 1995, p. 108). The Society of Netherlands Composers also withdrew their support from the protestors (Mineur 1989, p. 38).

The extensive press coverage subsequently received by the Nutcrackers was not simply due to the colourful nature of their exploits (which later involved occupying the Concertgebouw and sabotaging a concert held to mark a KLM Congress). At the 1969 Holland Festival, the single substantial creative endeavour of the Five – the musical 'morality' *Reconstructie* – had been a huge *succès de scandale*, and the best possible springboard for the first protest later that year. The interest of the public was sparked, not just by the spectacle of five composers and two librettists (Harry Mulisch and Hugo Claus) joining forces to produce a single work, but also by the highly topical subject matter – namely, Che Guevara and the capitalist exploitation of Latin America. *Reconstructie* combines several interleaved layers of narrative, including a pastiche 'reconstruction' of Mozart's *Don Giovanni*, in which the Commander (Guevara) avenges the honour of his daughter Bolivia; and a tale of 'big-time American businessmen' obstructed in their 'civilizing labours' in Latin America by the 'bandit' Plumed Serpent (Guevara once again).[23] At regular intervals throughout the piece, the chorus recites a litany of chilling statistics about the impact of US profiteering upon Latin America.

The direct (some might say crude) political message of *Reconstructie* certainly marked an advance on the uncommitted impression given by the music performed at the PDE concert. In other respects, however, it represented a continuation of the composers' – and particularly Andriessen's – compositional preoccupations. For instance, the practice of the PDE concert was repeated by pointedly avoiding a standard orchestra; instead, an ad hoc ensemble was assembled that included guitars and keyboards but no flutes, horns or violins. The Carré Theatre was again the venue, and resonances of the theatre's past can surely be felt in *Reconstructie*'s rather circus-like brand of 'total theatre', which involves dancers, actors and electronics as well as singers and musicians. Then there is the multi-stylistic quality of the music; its mixture of avant-garde, eighteenth-century classical, jazz, pop and folk styles directly extended the 'de-hierarchizing' of Andriessen's works of the preceding few years.

The stylistic schizophrenia of *Reconstructie* was probably not unconnected with the multiple authorship of the score, although, in a radical twist to the notion of the 'depersonification of the composer', it was an important principle that collective responsibility should be taken for all parts of the work: 'Each author was responsible for the entire work. No leader could be tolerated. It is like a guerilla movement, which can only be successful when based upon a firm unity of individual persons.'[24] Creative responsibility for the work did not stop with the five composers and two librettists. Extensive opportunities were given for some of the other illustrious performers to showcase their own talents: Frans Brüggen, Willem Breuker and the actor and singer Ramses Shaffy featured prominently in this panoply of Dutch musical talent. Little surprise that tickets were hot property (Peters 1994, p. 613).

Despite this, *Reconstructie* managed to stoke a long-running controversy, fanned by the conservative newspaper *De Telegraaf*, about the expenditure of public funds. The anti-Americanism of the work was the principal focus of indignation this time round; legend has it that *Reconstructie* was single-handedly responsible for deterring the newly elected Richard Nixon from

---

[23] Quotations are from the booklet accompanying the LP recording of *Reconstructie*.

[24] From W. Boswinkel, 'De achste man schrijft een opera', *Algemeen Handelsblad*, 21 September 1968. This statement notwithstanding, there were distinct areas of responsibility: according to Geert van Keulen, who played in the performances, Andriessen was solely responsible for the witty Mozart pastiche (private conversation).

visiting the Netherlands during a European tour (Vermeulen 1992, p. 15). However, anxiety over the general question of subsidy was later to be felt by some of the Nutcrackers themselves: the composer Bernard van Beurden, for instance, admitted that 'there is one problem. Our revolution is subsidized' (in De Beer 1994). Establishment patronage is famously prone to merge into establishment propaganda, and the Five could not entirely escape the charge that they ended up endorsing the social structures that they were attacking. Both the PDE concert and *Reconstructie* drew heavily on funds raised through general taxation, apparently for the primary benefit of the Amsterdam intelligentsia. Four years of subsidized protest had yielded little of concrete value for those not belonging to this initiated cultural class.[25]

A related difficulty made unavoidable by *Reconstructie* was the contradiction between the goal of a popular revolution and the musical practices used to espouse it. In spite of the flaunting of popular styles, *Reconstructie* remains a modernist product through and through. Its scoring for three orchestras and four conductors, each spatially distributed around the hall, is reminiscent of Stockhausen's *Carré* (maybe in homage to the venue of *Reconstructie*), and the abstruse musical language that prevails at the most serious moments of the work is generated by mysterious mathematical processes. (For instance, the composers inform us that borrowed material from *Don Giovanni* 'was processed according to our criteria by the computer into horizontal and vertical tone structures'.[26]) But the modernist qualities of the work are also reflected in the working relations between composers and performers. The intricacy of the composers' musical conception, which took little account of the preferences or pleasure of the performers, led to a strained working atmosphere during rehearsals (Schouten 1973, p. 63). The contradiction between the democratic idealism expressed in the libretto and

---

[25] In a letter to the author (13 February 2003), Andriessen has disputed this description of the relation of the Nutcrackers and governmental funds: 'We considered, and I do still consider, governmental support not a gift but a right. The money is not the property of the government; it is the people's own tax money, so it's your money you get back. Kids learn this in school when they learn about democracy.' But this does not answer the criticism that the 'people's own money' was not, in these cases, actually benefiting 'the people'.

[26] LP booklet. In a letter to the author (13 February 2003), Andriessen points out that the computers were no indication of lavish institutional support. 'At that time there was one computer available in Amsterdam for artistic research. Nobody had computers. We had to do all the computer programming ourselves and there did not exist any prefab software. So using a computer had absolutely nothing to do with being "established".'

the reality of the musicians' lot in realizing the piece vexed Andriessen in the long run, as we shall see. If the cause of revolution was to be pursued, it would require a different set of working relations and a different musical language.

Reconstruction

> These actions, they were – but now I speak only for myself – a sort of Abschied
> to official bourgeois musical life. (Andriessen, in Schouten 1973, p. 63)

If *Reconstructie* seemed to mark the end of an era, it was partly because of a more general shift in the political climate in the Netherlands at the start of the 1970s. James Kennedy has described how, at the start of the new decade, 'for many Dutch radicals, the *ludiek* approach now seemed a dead end' (Kennedy 1995, p. 268). As new ideas had become more widely accepted during the course of the previous few years, the need for theatrics and playful demonstrations diminished: now it was time for action. In the musical world this shift in emphasis was mirrored in a turn away from the Concertgebouw Orchestra as the focus of protest, and towards the establishment of meaningful and long-lasting alternatives. In March 1970, a group of over seventy composers (including the Five), musicians, musicologists and music students called a meeting at the experimental theatre De Brakke Grond to 'formulate an action programme' for 'a radical and democratic renewal of musical life'.[27] The agenda focused on the identification of 'concrete alternatives', and it ranged far beyond the relatively limited question of orchestral organization to address the possibility of identical funding for all musicians, an overhaul of educational provision at conservatories, and the opening up of all music-related decision-making to the public gaze.

The principal outcome of the meeting was the establishment of the 'Movement for the Renewal of Musical Practice' or BEVEM (Mineur 1989, p. 58 ff.). Of the many proposals to issue from this body, one of the most influential was the 'Plan for Ensembles'. This argued for a 'new definition of the concept of chamber music', one that would embrace unconventional groups of musicians 'formed more or less peripatetically', and which would recognize the need for greater financial support for this form of music-making (cited in Koopmans 1976b, p. 26). In so doing it laid the foundation for the institutionalized ensemble culture for which the Netherlands is renowned

---

[27] The 'Call to Meeting', which includes the agenda and list of signatories, is reproduced in Peters 1994, p. 614.

today, and on which the existence of works like *De Staat* are thoroughly dependent.

The 'peripatetic' ensembles to which the BEVEM plan refers had already become a feature of musical life in Amsterdam during 1970. In February a concert was organized by a cellist from (ironically) the Concertgebouw Orchestra, who invited musicians from all over the country as well as colleagues from the orchestra to perform in aid of the Netherlands-Vietnam Medical Committee (Van Royen 1989, pp. 135–36). A follow-up concert, entitled 'Musici voor Vietnam', took place eight months later at the same venue (Frascati, a former tobacco warehouse). Like its predecessor, this event combined musicians and ensembles from many different backgrounds playing music of their own choice; the formalities of traditional concert-giving were avoided, and entrance was free. Musici voor Vietnam became the first in a series of marathon 'Inclusief' concerts, in which the stylistic pluralism that had hitherto been confined to the 'quotation' works of the late sixties spilt out into actual concert practice. If 'high' and 'low' musics were traditionally associated with different social classes, then bringing them together on the level playing field of the Frascati or Carré theatres promised a more than theoretical social levelling.

Andriessen played a major role, alongside Reinbert de Leeuw and Willem Breuker, in the development of the Inclusief concerts (Schönberger 1975, p. 8). Compositionally, however, this was a time of uncertainty. In two large-scale works, *Hoe het is* ('How it is') (1969) and *Spektakel* (1970), Andriessen took an openly antagonistic attitude towards established performance traditions – writing, as he put it, 'against' classical musicians in each case (Andriessen 1977a, p. 139; Schouten 1974, p. 28). The crudely comic *Nine Symphonies of Beethoven for Promenade Orchestra and Ice Cream Bell* is a more entertaining debunking exercise, in which excerpts from the symphonies and other works are sewn together with snippets of Italian-style symphonic pop. The work was a great public success at its first performance, but Andriessen found himself less than amused:

> It was a truly disgusting, commercialized, weird mess with all sorts of gags and jokes. *Für Elise*, the 'Moonlight' Sonata – nothing was beyond my reach in that piece. When I stood there on the podium and [the conductor] Gijsbert Nieuwland shook hands with me, I thought: there is something utterly wrong with me, and if I'm not careful things are going to end up very badly. I think that that was one of the moments when I was totally chastened. (In Schouten 1974, pp. 27–28)[28]

---

[28] Compare the account in Andriessen 1972, p. 130.

A month later, the first performance in the Concertgebouw of a new version of *Spektakel*, in which Willem Breuker was given free reign to incorporate longer sections of improvisation and theatrical tomfoolery into the original's 'confrontation of musical worlds',[29] aroused similarly ambivalent feelings: 'That was certainly a nice evening, but a critic wrote that it was a scandal that this could happen in the Concertgebouw. Suddenly I understood: yes, I do not belong here any more. These sorts of things are also not at home here. I have to know my place' (ibid., p. 28). Andriessen had come to the realization that a satirical attitude towards established musical traditions in itself offered little future for his own music, and that the principal outlets for composed music – specifically, concert hall and orchestra – could no longer be reconciled with his creative and ideological outlook. He found himself completely alienated from the culture that had nurtured him as a musician.

The result of this predicament was a full year – most of 1971 – in which he composed next to nothing, and instead (as he later recalled) 'just stayed at home, sitting on the sofa, thinking about the meaning of composing' (Andriessen, in Andriessen and Schönberger 1981, p. 8). He felt unable to write music. His frustration was partly a question of class politics: 'I detest that class of ladies and gentlemen who consume the music which affirms their self-satisfied social status' (Andriessen 1972, p. 129). But it was also driven by a kind of musical ethics. Specifically, Andriessen recoiled from institutions – above all, the orchestra – that deprived musicians of meaningful choice and freedom. An orchestral piece like *Anachronie I*, however progressive its musical techniques might be, was

> already alienated from the producers: the orchestral musicians. The piece was dumped on the musicians' music stands, they had to do what Sir said and after two rehearsals and one concert it disappeared in the cupboard. No one understood *what* he had played and *why*. And nobody gave a damn. I could hear (and see) *that* by the way they played. (Ibid., p. 128)

From this perspective, 'the free, unbound, you could say anarchistic attitude' of jazz and popular music was positively enlightened: 'What attracted me there is the authenticity, that what people play comes from themselves. They don't do what Sir says; they do what they find best' (Andriessen, in Schouten 1974, p. 28). Andriessen remained suspicious, though, of the commercial forces underlying much pop music, and remained convinced that music ought

---

[29] Andriessen, in programme booklet for this performance of *Spektakel* (stored in the Gaudeamus Foundation Library).

to command the listener's sustained attention. The fields of pop and 'light' jazz offered no solution for him personally.[30]

However, two other types of music promised a similar kind of liberation for the performer *and* possessed the radical edge that Andriessen found instinctively attractive. In the course of 1971, stimuli from the fields of improvisation and American minimalism combined to suggest a way forward for his own music. Improvisation had been an important part of the Dutch music scene since the mid-sixties. Although initially associated with jazz, improvisation eventually gained a distinct identity of its own, partly on the back of the Fluxus and performance art movements that had flourished so successfully in the Netherlands. From 1967, the Instant Composers Pool acted as an umbrella organization for improvisers, and it – and particularly the ICP events directed by Andriessen's colleague and collaborator Willem Breuker – became a crucial model for Andriessen's ideal of music-making:

> In the Netherlands there were only a few musicians who played music which was really their own intellectual property ...: these were the Instant Composers Pool under the inspirational direction of Willem Breuker. The instinctively anti-bourgeois manner of their playing ... had already attracted me for a long time. I wanted to work with musicians who could play nothing other than that which was, or would become, their (musical) property and who would call for work of high quality. (Andriessen 1972, p. 129)

Andriessen was also influenced at this time by figures from the world of electronic improvisation, particularly Dick Raaijmakers and Gilius van Bergeijk. Raaijmakers and Van Bergeijk found new audiences by performing in museums and galleries rather than conventional concert venues, and they were critical of the obsession with traditional musical institutions and the 'épater le bourgeois' attitude of the Nutcrackers (Schouten 1973, p. 65). Their music was 'conceptual' – which is to say, it was as much about the idea generating the work as the finished properties of that work – but it was also simple and direct: easy for anyone to comprehend. *Volkslied* ['National Anthem'] for any melody instrument, one of the few short pieces Andriessen wrote during 1971, shows the impact of this approach. It comprises the Dutch national anthem, repeated over and over but with progressively more notes altered until the melody has completely metamorphosed into the 'Internationale' – the anthem of the communist movement. (The transformation was determined by a computer program.) Years later, Andriessen suggested that all his works from the 1970s can be considered 'conceptual

---

[30] I discuss Andriessen's attitude to popular culture in Ch. 2.

music' (Andriessen, in Gronemeyer 1992, p. 54). The reductive simplicity of
the purest kind of conceptual music is missing in a piece like *De Staat*, but the
continuing importance of an orientation towards generating ideas as much as
end products should certainly not be underestimated.

The second major stimulus for Andriessen at this time came from American
minimalism. In 1970, Frederic Rzewski introduced Andriessen to the then-
recent recording of Terry Riley's *In C* (Trochimczyk (ed.) 2002, p. 20).[31] This
was to be the pivotal event in Andriessen's encounter with minimalism – an
encounter that will be discussed in greater detail in the next chapter. The
appeal of *In C* was not unrelated to that of improvisation: in spite of its
'composed' nature, it allows considerable freedom for each individual
musician, who decides how many times to repeat each of the work's 53
modules. This 'democratic' attitude to performers is coupled, moreover, to a
musical idiom that is both radical and accessible. Andriessen realized that a
socially engaged music demanded a retreat from the forbidding abstractions of
the avant-garde: as he later summarized the situation, 'seeing revolution on the
streets, I realized that my choice [of musical style] had to involve the
musicians and the world' (Schwarz 1996, p. 205). Minimalism offered an
immediacy and physicality that connected it to pop, yet retained a
conceptualist element that helped distinguish it from the world of commercial
music – a crucial distinction for a leftist composer hostile to the corporate
world.

American minimalism also emulated jazz and improvisation by involving
the composer in the performance of his works: Riley featured on the recording
of *In C*, and by 1968 Steve Reich and Philip Glass had both established
ensembles featuring themselves as performers as well as composers. It was
this idea that formed the immediate spur for the composition of *De Volharding*
('Perseverance') towards the end of 1971, and that led to the creation of the
ensemble of the same name. Andriessen conceived 'a piece with jazz licks, a
sort of piano concerto with a whole load of wind instruments' (Andriessen
1996b, p. 116).[32] He turned to Willem Breuker in order to assemble the
musicians: 'We telephoned the cast together: Willem rounded up jazz men

---

[31] Sources – and presumably Andriessen's memory – differ as to the date of this.
Elsewhere the date is given as 1971 (Schwarz 1996, p. 206) or 1969 (Koning and
Jansen 1981, p. 15).

[32] Writing in 1972, Andriessen notes that, besides minimalism and jazz, other
inspiration was provided by 'Stravinsky's Piano Concerto, the Bach suites, *Eclat* by
Boulez and Japanese gagaku'; see Andriessen 1972, p. 131. This article, drawn from
Andriessen's personal notebooks, is the definitive statement on the founding, aesthetic
rationale and early repertoire of the Orkest De Volharding.

who could read well and I phoned young classical musicians who were up for doing something strange' (ibid., p. 117). The original band comprised three saxophones, three trumpets and three trombones, in addition to Andriessen on the piano. Rehearsals began in January 1972, and much of the creative work was done by the other musicians: 'I was not going to contribute more than a few indications of the style; the content of the piece needed to come into being in the rehearsals' (Andriessen 1972, p. 131). It was consistent with the spirit of the venture that the idea of a public performance arose only as something of an afterthought (Whitehead 1999, p. 89).

Following a trial run of part of the work on 30 April at a protest meeting against the Vietnam war, the full version was premiered on 12 May in the Carré Theatre at what turned out to be the last of the marathon Inclusief concerts. The performance became a famous occasion in Dutch musical life. It was not until shortly before midnight that the musicians took the stage, and as the recording of the performance shows, it soon aroused a noisy reaction from the audience. Shouts of derision – caused partly by the work's insistent repetitiveness, partly by its continuously loud volume and partly by the abrasive style of performance – were met with yells of support and, ultimately, a rowdy ovation. (This work and the others written by Andriessen for the Orkest De Volharding are assessed in greater detail in the next chapter.) The uproar probably contributed to most of the performers' decision that they should continue as an ensemble. So, with the addition of a flautist, a horn player and a double bassist, the Orkest De Volharding was born.

Andriessen's period of reflection on 'the meaning of composing' had enabled him to formulate what might be called an ideology of musical practice, of which De Volharding was to be the living embodiment – and which was to remain central for him up to and beyond the composition of *De Staat*. The outlines of this ideology are clear from the manifesto De Volharding circulated to potential venues:

> The repertoire of the Orkest De Volharding is assembled by the group itself, the point of departure being a critical attitude in respect of prevailing musical practice. That has an influence on the way the orchestra plays (it consists of jazz musicians and musicians with a classical training) and the places where they play. It hopes to sever the links that exist between certain music, performance conventions and listeners by making a conscious choice with regard to repertoire and the style of playing. Also, according to the circumstances in which De Volharding plays (on the street, in club houses, at universities) it reaches a different and new public, which it directly involves in the production of the music by taking as a point of departure their existing taste, developing it and criticizing it. (Cited in Schouten 1974, p. 30)

Foremost in De Volharding's critical attitude to conventional musical practice was the question of working relations. Andriessen never again wanted to find himself in the situation where performers played his music against their will:

> Everyone must be at one with each note. The music must be the property of the guys who play. It should not be that as the composer you are the employer and they are the employees. You must take care that they know what they are playing, and why, and for whom. (Andriessen, in Van Marissing 1973)

This requirement found itself manifested in a number of different ways. Composers of new pieces for the band had to remain open to the musical preferences of the musicians, to the extent that 'the musicians take part in the composing' (ibid.). On a more symbolic level, De Volharding played without conductor and performed standing shoulder to shoulder, every individual as important as the next. And their performing style – famously idiosyncratic in terms of intonation and ensemble – not only refuted the traditional refinement of classical performers, but was justified on the basis that each player was playing the way he or she wanted.

Realigning the relationship of performer and composer (or, as De Volharding publicity preferred to put it, 'conception' and 'production') dealt with one half of the musical equation. Realigning production and 'consumption' was equally vital. A balancing act was necessary here, between the accessibility necessary to communication with new audiences, and the critical attitude that made simply satisfying people's existing musical tastes unacceptable. At one level, greater accessibility was a straightforward matter of leaving behind the concert hall and seeking alternative venues. De Volharding played in cafés, church halls, community halls, universities and conservatoires, and, almost exclusively to begin with, at political meetings. But there was also the need to break completely with the obscure experimentalism that could still be detected in pieces like *Hoe het is* and *Spektakel*. A Volharding brochure issued in 1972 declared that, 'We no longer consider … experimental [musical] research to be experimental. The quality of pure esthetic research can, we believe, be gauged only through social application' (cited in Koopmans 1976b, p. 27). This statement directly echoes the sentiments of the German composer and writer Hanns Eisler, who had already insisted during the 1920s that the progressiveness of a musical composition could not be detached from its social functioning:

> The modern composer must learn to grasp that the solution of the crisis in music no longer depends on his talent, but can be brought about only by remedying the more general social crisis. Therefore it is necessary that the composer seek a

certain social framework, in which he produces and experiments. He must seek
a social position. (Eisler, in Van Marissing 1973)

Eisler was of great importance to Andriessen in the early days of De
Volharding. Andriessen viewed him as 'probably the first composer to be
aware of the connection that exists between musical conception (composition), production (performance) and the consumption of music' (Andriessen
1975, p. 430). As a composer with a background in the avant-garde (Eisler had
studied with Schoenberg) who had subsequently experienced a social
awakening and eventually rejected the musical idiom of his youth, Eisler's
development foreshadowed Andriessen's. However, Andriessen's interest in
Eisler extended to a more direct involvement with his music. During 1972
Andriessen worked with Paul Binnerts at the Amsterdam Theatre School on a
student production of Brecht's '*Lehrstück*' *Die Massnahme* ('The Measures
Taken'); in place of Eisler's original music Andriessen wrote new settings
for piano and unison choir 'in the spirit of Eisler' (Koopmans 1982,
pp. 12, 46).[33] The 'new sort of speech-song style' that he developed for the production's untrained singers was to be of lasting importance to his approach to
text-setting, as we will see in Chapter 4. Eisler's well-known *Solidaritätslied*
(1931) also became a kind of signature tune for De Volharding. It is not too
difficult to hear the influence of the pervasive striding rhythms of Eisler's
political music in Andriessen's *De Volharding*, or for that matter in *De
Staat*.

One of Eisler's central tenets during the 1920s was that abstract
instrumental music was hopelessly outdated, nothing more than a temporary
obsession of the nineteenth-century bourgeoisie. The future lay instead in
angewandte Musik, or 'applied music', which in practice meant music for the
theatre, cinema, cabaret or public events. This attitude was strongly influential
on both the Orkest De Volharding and Andriessen personally. In the first
couple of years of its existence De Volharding prioritized political gatherings
over 'bourgeois concerts' (Koopmans 1982, p. 48): they appeared at Vietnam
protest meetings, meetings of the General Students Union and the Communist
Party, and demonstrations against car pollution and the Chilean military
coup.[34] There were also collaborations with new experimental theatre
companies: they played some jazzy incidental music written by Andriessen for

---

[33] Andriessen wrote an article about his music for this production: see Andriessen
1975.

[34] Koopmans's book lists all De Volharding performances during the first ten years
of its existence.

the Sater theatre group; and Breuker's music for the Baal theatre group's inaugural production of Brecht's *Baal* was played by De Volharding in all but name (Koopmans 1982, p. 26; Whitehead 1999, pp. 82, 85). Andriessen himself, when not playing with De Volharding, wrote the soundtrack for Lodewijk de Boer's film *The Family* – a score that proves he could easily have made a living as a commercial film composer – and began teaching at the Hague Conservatory. From early 1976, he took over from Breuker as principal resident composer for the Baal theatre group.[35]

The 'usefulness' for which De Volharding strove was not at the expense of a critical edge and an insistence on developing audiences. This was consistent with Eisler, too. Eisler had been fearful of the way in which the cultural products of modern society encouraged the passive listener and 'the blunting of the intellect of the masses'; a composer had a responsibility to engage with society precisely in order 'to clarify the consciousness of the most advanced class, the working class' (Eisler 1978, pp. 111, 116). Thus it was important that all pieces in the early repertoire of De Volharding should 'take a radical standpoint with regard to generally accepted material' (Andriessen, in Van Marissing 1973). Beside the political songs, arrangements of Milhaud's *La Création du monde* and Stravinsky's *Tango* featured prominently in early De Volharding concerts. What interested Andriessen about these works was not just the precedent they set in combining classical and jazz styles, but also the sense in which they provided a critique upon the musics they incorporate (Andriessen 1972, p. 134). It was important that new pieces for the ensemble, too, should 'pass critical comment on prevailing musical forms and musical practices', though this should not take the form of 'abstract rejection, formulated as if from outside; rather, the critique comes from an engagement with what you criticize' (Andriessen, in Van Marissing 1973).

The emphasis on critique chimed with Andriessen's and Breuker's extensive involvement with Brechtian theatre during the early seventies. Brecht's concept of the Lehrstück ('learning-piece') – in the development of which Eisler had played a crucial role – provided a particularly appealing model for a form of musical performance aimed at critical engagement rather than cosy escapism. Its openly didactic intention found a reflection in the spoken introductions that were 'an integral part' of Volharding performances

---

[35] Andriessen had already composed extensively for the theatre prior to this period. Between 1968 and 1972 he wrote music for over a dozen theatre productions. Records for many of these can be found on the website of the Theater Instituut Nederland (<http://www.tin.nl>).

(Koopmans 1982, p. 40). And the importance attached to discussion in the Lehrstück was also emulated in attempts to initiate post-performance discussions – although audiences were not always equally enthusiastic (see Schouten 1974, p. 30). De Volharding performances often resembled Eisler's description of the Lehrstück as 'a special kind of political seminar' (cited in Brecht 1997, p. xv). As we will see in Chapter 4, the idea of the Lehrstück and other Brechtian principles of theatre were of lasting importance for Andriessen, not least in relation to *De Staat*.

Breuker left De Volharding in 1974, but Andriessen remained its pianist until September 1976, two months before the premiere of *De Staat*. He explained to the *Groene Amsterdammer* that he had grown weary of the incessant touring of the performing musician, but also that 'I have much more to do on the musical side. I have the feeling that I have to say things that are more complicated, because some things simply *are* more complicated' (in Steenhuis and Wijtman 1976, p. 3). Even then, he remained completely committed to his vocation as an 'applied composer' through his relationship with the theatre group Baal and his establishment of and participation in the student ensemble Hoketus. In 1976, Elmer Schönberger wrote that 'Louis Andriessen operates in the margins of musical life' (Schönberger 1976, p. 38), a fact that is difficult to appreciate today given Andriessen's renown and eminence, but is crucially important to a full understanding of *De Staat*.

Andriessen's persistent efforts to overcome traditional social barriers in the musical world were in keeping with developments in the wider social sphere. The mid-seventies in the Netherlands witnessed the cementing of the 'inclusive society' that was to dominate the country's modern image in the eyes of the rest of the world. Many of the reforms for which the Provos fought in the 1960s became a reality in legislation designed to recognize individuals' rights to pursue their own preferences and lifestyles (Newton 1978, p. 204). But was everything as it seemed in this period of liberalization? James Kennedy has argued that the Netherlands' cultural revolution was managed by a group of leaders more interested in power than progressive politics; visible social reform tended to deflect attention from the continuing importance of conservative bourgeois values and lifestyles in Dutch life and culture (Kennedy 1995, p. 4). That there remained an underlying resistance to wholesale change, eye-catching reforms notwithstanding, is suggested by the continuing dominance in musical life of the symphony orchestra. By 1976 the number of orchestras in the Netherlands had grown to an all-time high of 21. And national subsidies for orchestras remained at roughly the same level at the end of the 1970s as they had been at the beginning – around 80 per cent of the total music budget.[36] Throughout the decade, Andriessen remained loudly critical of the continuing power of the symphony orchestra in musical life, and, despite the ongoing generosity of governmental support for orchestras, certain that change was inevitable:

> Those 21 orchestras that all play the same stuff must change from the inside. I am absolutely convinced that I will still be around when there are only one or two symphony orchestras left in the Netherlands, and in addition to that an enormous variety of activity. I am convinced that that will happen and I will contribute something to that myself, I promise. (Andriessen, in Steenhuis and Wijtman 1976, pp. 3–4)

It was in this context that *De Staat* was first performed on 26 November 1976.

---

[36] The figures are taken from the annual budget statements of the Ministerie van Cultuur, Recreatie en Maatschappelijk Werk, copies of which are housed in the Boekmanstichting, Amsterdam.

Chapter 2

Jazz, Minimalism and Stravinsky

The purpose of this chapter is twofold. It considers some of the principal musical influences on Andriessen's music of the 1970s. And it provides an introduction to some of the works that immediately precede *De Staat*, many of which were written for the Orkest De Volharding. Andriessen has never sought to disguise the impact made by existing music upon his own composition; the importance of jazz, minimalism and Stravinsky in particular is profound and multifaceted. However, he himself resists use of the word 'influence'. In his music, references to other music are a very conscious point of principle. They are, he suggests, deliberate 'structural allusions',[1] and not, as the word 'influence' sometimes implies, more involuntary genetic traits. The distinction is a revealing one, not least because the suspicion of influence aligns him with the post-war avant-garde, who generally sought to portray their music as coming into existence *ab nihilo*. Unlike the products of the modernist avant-garde, though, Andriessen's music loudly proclaims its connections with existing models; whether it counts as 'influence' or not, we will see that the impact of other musics extends well beyond 'structural' considerations to encompass approaches to performance and attitudes regarding meaning and expression. Andriessen concedes that his attitude to other music in itself betrays a constant guiding presence: 'it does not matter if it's jazz, gagaku or C. P. E. Bach. The fact that there are structural allusions to other music is a result of the influence of Stravinsky.'[2]

An assessment of Stravinsky's importance for Andriessen closes this chapter, where there will be more to say on the general question of 'music about music'. As with the preceding sections, only the roughest of sketches can be offered here, but this should be sufficient to indicate the distinctive combination of ingredients that makes Andriessen's music so individual and appealing. Surveying the works that precede *De Staat* serves a further purpose. For all that the music of the early 1970s merits attention in its own right, it provides little forewarning of the scale and ambition of *De Staat*. Here,

---

[1] Letter to the author (4 April 2003).
[2] Ibid.

Andriessen draws together the various styles and idioms explored in previous works, but in a way that consolidates those elements that are more fully his own. It is this quality – the transcending of 'structural allusions', even as the music continues openly to acknowledge that it is always inevitably 'about other music' (Andriessen, in Van Rossum and Smit 1994, p. 15) – that allows Elmer Schönberger to identify *De Staat* as marking 'the birth of the "true" Louis Andriessen' (Schönberger 1996, p. 13).

Jazz

> Dutch compositions, you see, all tend towards jazz a little – they're physical, they're harder. (Andriessen, in Koopmans 1976b, p. 36)

Louis Andriessen's renown in Britain and the United States is based on his reputation as a 'crossover' composer. Young classically trained composers interested in incorporating elements of pop, rock or jazz in their compositions have long regarded him as a trail-blazer in this respect.[3] But Andriessen's interest in combining classical music and jazz reflects a general susceptibility to cross-fertilization – Gisela Gronemeyer refers to a 'symbiotic relationship' (Gronemeyer 1992, p. 55) – between these two genres in the Netherlands. Willem Breuker, Misha Mengelberg and Theo Loevendie, all prominent figures in the field of improvisation during the sixties, also wrote fully composed music, both for jazz musicians and for the classical concert hall. Younger musicians such as Maarten Altena, Guus Janssen and Peter van Bergen have continued this tradition of bridging jazz and classical worlds. Institutions such as the Amsterdam Concertgebouw hall, which hosted jazz concerts from the fifties onwards, helped facilitate the recognition of jazz as a serious art form (Whitehead 1999, pp. 6, 11, 29, 42). By the mid-seventies the Netherlands had an unparalleled system of institutional support for jazz and improvisation, with dedicated subsidies from city and state, jazz departments in the music conservatories, and a state-funded venue for jazz performance (the BIMhuis in Amsterdam) (ibid., pp. 72 ff., 102–5). The creation of the Orkest De Volharding was only possible because of the relatively high status of jazz musicians in the Netherlands, and the already well-established interactions between them and classical musicians (ibid., pp. 58–59, 226–27).

---

[3] Thus the composers Michael Gordon, David Lang and Julia Wolfe, who founded the trendy Bang on a Can Festival in downtown Manhattan in the late 1980s, have declared that 'Andriessen changed our lives for ever' (back cover of Andriessen 2002).

Andriessen himself had an early exposure to jazz, as we saw in Chapter 1. Aside from the influence of his brother, he made friends with a number of jazz musicians at the Hague Conservatory: these included Misha Mengelberg, Boudewijn Leeuwenberg and Hans van Sweeden (Bernlef 1981). Early enthusiasms ranged across boogie-woogie, big band and bebop: Andriessen has singled out Albert Ammons, Pete Johnson, Jimmy Yancey, Count Basie, Stan Kenton, Dizzy Gillespie and Charlie Parker amongst others (Witts 1978, De Beer 1985, Andriessen 1990b). These were later joined by complementary tastes for the more radical 'free' jazz of Anthony Braxton and George Lewis on the one hand, and the 'glossy women's magazine' music (to adopt Andriessen's politically incorrect description) of Michel Legrand and the Swingle Singers on the other (Whitehead 1999, p. 243; Koopmans 1976b, p. 36).

Andriessen's wide-ranging taste in jazz and 'light' music has sometimes been taken as signifying a general enthusiasm for popular culture – an image that was to prove highly marketable as the fashion for crossover music gained momentum during the eighties and nineties. His activities in the 1970s certainly appeared consistent with a taste for all things popular. The 'Inclusive Concerts' which Andriessen helped to organize featured jazz and pop alongside classical avant-garde; and, as we have seen, the Orkest De Volharding took the 'music of the people' as its primary point of reference. Both of these initiatives had the aim of overcoming the traditional association between certain sorts of music and certain social classes. 'De-hierarchizing' was the buzzword of the time; the incorporation of a pop group to accompany the 'Ode to Joy' at the end of *The Nine Symphonies of Beethoven* symbolized the eradication of the distinction between 'high' and 'low' musics. Andriessen's later expressions of approval for black soul and disco (Schwarz 1996, p. 208; Hulsman 1995) helped to cement the 'hip' image.

But, as a closer reading of Andriessen's endorsement of black popular music reveals, this image in fact belies a more complex relationship to popular culture, one that Andriessen has never been afraid to articulate publicly. He has enthused about the music of Janet Jackson, for instance, but he describes it as 'more related to jazz than pop music' (Andriessen, in Hulsman 1995), and this wariness in relation to the category of 'pop' is a common theme throughout his statements on popular culture. His suspicion of the commercial aspects of pop music was, as I suggested in Chapter 1, an inevitable consequence of his politicized antipathy to large-scale corporate interests. Fascinatingly, though, Andriessen also remained immune at this time to more progressive and politically aware pop. He found the Beatles 'primitive', for instance, in spite of their musical innovations (see Ford 1993, p. 82). And as for political music, 'what the students and Provos "stirred" on the street, we [i.e. the Five] heard not so much in Joan Baez or Bob Dylan as in Ornette Coleman, Charles Ives and Erik Satie' (Andriessen 1995b, p. 109). Andriessen continued to express distaste for pop music throughout the 1970s. The idea of involving pop musicians in the Orkest De Volharding, for instance, was out of the question: 'No pop musicians. 90 per cent work exclusively for the money and 99 per cent cannot read music. You make it too easy for yourself if you throw that whole discipline overboard. Then it interests me much less' (Andriessen, in Schouten 1974, p. 28). In 1975, with scant regard for overstatement, Andriessen pronounced the pioneer commercial pop music station Radio Veronica 'a disaster for mankind' (in Krook 1976).

Andriessen found Veronica so disturbing partly because of his aversion – shared by many in 'cultured' sectors of society – to the 'sound pollution' caused by the ubiquity of recorded music in modern life (Op de Coul 1979). This threatened a principle central to Andriessen's musical upbringing: namely, that music 'was for listening to …: it was taken very seriously' (Andriessen and Schönberger 1979, p. 14). For Andriessen, 'the constant presence of music everywhere … detracts from good listening', a situation that made him 'very pessimistic' (in Op de Coul 1979). And much pop music seemed to invite this sort of distracted engagement in the very way in which it is constructed. In a line of argument entirely consistent with Theodor Adorno's well-known critique of pop music,[4] Andriessen has expressed dislike of both the simple structures of pop music ('I do not like pop music very much because I find it too light, too simple'; in Trochimczyk (ed.) 2002, p. 21) and its tendencies towards mindlessness (the drum-kit, in particular, giving rise to 'the automatism … [of] pop music'; in Whitehead 1999, p. 79). Pop music may demonstrate '*remnants* of authentic musical qualities', but these are in spite of rather than because of its '"commodity"-character' (Andriessen 1975, p. 443).

In this context, Andriessen's interest in jazz signals not so much a laissez-faire attitude to the 'music of the people' as a perception that jazz is something fundamentally different from pop. While jazz may have been 'lowbrow',[5] it was not 'light' music; on the contrary, it was 'the folk music which is musically the most developed' (Andriessen 1972, p. 131). Even when it lacked structural sophistication, it remained stimulating and provocative in its attitude to performance – the energy, character and sporadic vulgarity of which

---

[4] For an accessible summary of this critique, see Robert W. Witkin, *Adorno on Music* (London: Routledge, 1998).

[5] This is the implication of a remark cited in Schwarz 1996, p. 206.

contrasted refreshingly with classical performance styles. In fact, while (as we will see) Andriessen's music has drawn fruitfully on a number of structural characteristics of jazz, it is the approach of jazz musicians to *performance* that has been of greatest consequence.

A number of Andriessen's compositions allude explicitly to jazz. For instance, *De Stijl* (1985) chronicles Piet Mondrian's love of boogie-woogie with the help of a substantial solo turn for honky-tonk pianist. In *Facing Death* (1990), Andriessen tackles the seemingly impossible task of transferring the bebop style of Charlie Parker to a string quartet. Jazz-influenced film music styles feature prominently in the music-theatre piece *Rosa* (1994), which relates the life and death of the film composer Juan Manuel de Rosa. The forerunner to all of these, though, was the second substantial piece that Andriessen wrote for the Orkest De Volharding in 1973. Its title, *On Jimmy Yancey*, refers to one of the foremost boogie-woogie pianists of the twenties and thirties. Andriessen's homage falls into two short movements: the first quotes three Yancey numbers, each of which is halted mid-way; the second is 'a kind of In Memoriam',[6] characterized by a slow, sustained melody over chugging boogie-woogie bass rhythms. Both movements end with the characteristic closing phrase that Yancey used to finish all his recordings.

On Jimmy Yancey thus includes a number of features that refer directly to Yancey himself. But it also helped to cement those aspects of Andriessen's newly evolving, post-avant-garde idiom that were derived from jazz, and which are carried over into later works. In terms of harmony this is partly a matter of 'blue notes' – the lowered third, seventh or (less frequently) fifth degree of the diatonic scale commonly found in blues and jazz. Blue thirds and fifths abound at the start of *On Jimmy Yancey*, not least in the very first chord, which consists simply of flattened third and flattened fifth. The flattened seventh is later startlingly highlighted in combination with the flattened third, in a harmonic jolt lifted direct from Yancey's 1939 track 'South Side Stuff'.[7] This use of additional notes to complicate a basic diatonic (or white-note) scale[8] – often, as we will see in the following chapter, specifically the blue

---

[6] Composer's programme note (Muziekgroep Nederland archive).

[7] See the seventh bar after [5] in *On Jimmy Yancey*. 'South Side Stuff' is included on Jimmy Yancey, *Complete Recorded Works Vol. 1 (1939–1940)* (Document, DOCD-5041).

[8] A diatonic scale is any seven-note scale that incorporates five whole-tone steps and two semitone steps, the latter being separated by two and three whole tones respectively. Any seven adjacent notes on the white keys of the keyboard will produce a diatonic scale.

notes common in jazz – remains common in Andriessen's later music. Rhythmically, the first movement of *On Jimmy Yancey* predictably makes a feature of syncopated rhythms, with sustained notes placed just ahead of the beat and numerous accented off-beat interjections. However, it also establishes a schism, reproduced in later works of the seventies, between passages with authentically jazzy rhythms and others characterized by the more earth-bound, marching style of Hanns Eisler. The final section of the first movement and the whole of the second movement conform more to the latter, the ever-present boogie-inspired ostinati deprived of any compensating rhythmic whimsy in the other parts, and correspondingly made rather arduous. (The original recording by the Orkest De Volharding suggests that the music is in no small degree reliant on the thick, intense tone of Willem Breuker's alto sax, which drives the sustained melodic lines forward with great ardour.[9]) This polarity between hot syncopation and hard slog is, if anything, intensified in *De Staat*, the music careering unpredictably between the contrasting worlds of big band and Bertolt Brecht.

The big-band tradition is also important to *On Jimmy Yancey*, despite its ostensible focus on an earlier phase of jazz history. Indeed, of all jazz, it was 'the big-band culture: the writing, settings, arrangements, the harmonies of large groups of brass instruments' that Andriessen believes has been most significant for his music (Andriessen, in Trochimczyk (ed.) 2002, p. 20).[10] The original Orkest De Volharding corresponded to the standard line-up of Count Basie's or Duke Ellington's swing bands in the late thirties and early forties, which comprised three to five each of trumpets, trombones and saxophones, and a four-part rhythm section (piano, bass, guitar and drums). The crucial difference is the lack of percussion in De Volharding's 'rhythm section', which comprises simply piano and bass.[11] In fact, during the 1970s percussion kept a low profile in Andriessen's music generally – a striking situation given the 'virtually indispensable' role played by percussion in jazz (Kernfeld 1995, p. 159). The focus on brass and winds in the Volharding works and beyond, however, remains a clear reflection of jazz traditions. Andriessen's treatment of these instrumental resources also shows the influence of big-band scoring. The first movement of *On Jimmy Yancey*, for instance, juxtaposes and contrasts the distinct instrumental groups, prioritizes homophonic writing over counterpoint, and delights in sudden brash gestures for the whole

---

[9] Released on LP in 1975 as Volharding 002.

[10] See also Whitehead 1999, p. 241.

[11] This was partly due to Willem Breuker, who had been 'traumatized' by years of working with the temperamental drummer Han Bennink; see Whitehead 1997, p. 6.

band.[12] All of these big-band traits can also be found in *De Staat*: sometimes idiomatically, as with the noisy brass entry at bar 403 or the dense homophonic scoring from bar 823;[13] sometimes in a more stylized fashion, as with the brusque contrasts of instrumental groups at the opening, or the parallel chord progressions from bar 889. The exciting cross-rhythms between bar 702 and bar 724 are essentially a reinterpretation of the effect achieved by Count Basie from layering different syncopated riffs in reeds, brass and rhythm sections (Kernfeld 1995, p. 91).

Andriessen's reception of jazz did not stop with questions of harmony, rhythm or scoring. He was also interested in the way that jazz musicians performed. There were two, interrelated aspects to this: first, the way in which jazz performance style offered an alternative to the 'bourgeois' performance style of the symphony orchestra; and second, the way in which jazz performance seemed to reflect directly, and thus 'authentically', the personality of the individual performer. An early indication of Andriessen's interest is provided by the first version of *Ittrospezione III* (1964), in which the solo saxophone – a part written with Willem Breuker in mind – is instructed to play with a 'brutal and hard sound (like in jazz)'. The raw, unblended tone, varying intonation, and 'between the eyes' style of Breuker's ICP players reflected well-established practices in jazz performance,[14] and was highly attractive to Andriessen, as we saw in the last chapter. Thus, 'the way in which you place your finger on the key or stick the reed in your mouth' was, from the start, a crucial issue for De Volharding (Andriessen, in Van Marissing 1973). Indeed the scores of the works written for De Volharding, like most jazz scores, give a less than adequate representation of the music, for their impact was considerably dependent on the performance characteristics of the musicians: on the powerful tone and improvisatory squalls of Breuker; on the heavy treatment meted out to the upright piano by Andriessen; on the looseness of ensemble and other 'inaccuracies' that were almost an article of faith for the whole band.

A suspicion of standard classical performance technique has remained with Andriessen ever since the Volharding years. It was to prove a problem with an early performance of *De Staat* in Warsaw, for instance, in which the orchestral

---

[12] Compare the descriptions of big-band scoring in Gridley 2000, p. 92 and Kernfeld 1995, pp. 76–88.

[13] CD timings corresponding to *De Staat*'s bar numbers are contained in Appendix B.

[14] On these characteristics of jazz, see Kernfeld 1995, p. 165; Gridley 2000, p. 407; Jackson 2002, p. 89.

musicians 'articulated the piece like Bruckner and Mahler. And it should be articulated like Count Basie and Stan Kenton!' (Andriessen 1990b, p. 149). One way to understand what Andriessen means by this is that his music requires attention to be shifted away from the *continuation* of notes – which tends to be prioritized in standard classical performance – to focus on their initial attack. In this respect the piano forms the principal orchestrational model, as it did, arguably, for Stravinsky (Andriessen and Schönberger 1989, p. 146). In *De Staat*, as in other works from the 1970s, fortepianos, accents, and markings of non-legato, portato (meaning 'detached') and non-vibrato abound.

Andriessen's attitude to singing also reflects these priorities. His antipathy to the classically trained 'bel canto' voice, which traditionally prioritizes tone-quality and volume over textual intelligibility, is well known. The vibrato of the classical voice is a particular *bête noire*:

> I am very specifically a sworn enemy of vibrato. It is not necessary anymore: it is not done by Baroque singers, it is not done by jazz singers, it is not done by folk singers, it is not done by pop singers, and it is not done by mothers when they sing to their children. Such a vibrato is not done by anybody else and it is a very unnatural, 'manneristic' way of making a sound. (Andriessen, in Trochimczyk (ed.) 2002, p. 169)[15]

Besides objecting to the sound itself, Andriessen finds the classical voice 'rather "posh"' (ibid.) – and thus out of place in music that seeks to embrace a wider audience. This may seem an arbitrary characterization, but Andriessen is not alone in viewing the classical voice in this way. In his study of vocal styles, John Potter proposes that the 'bel canto' voice has been the principal 'ideological flag-bearer of bourgeois music making' since the late nineteenth century, through its emphasis on training and technique, and its distinctness from all other types of singing (Potter 1998, pp. 63–64, 193). Other composers have, like Andriessen, eagerly sought alternatives to it. In *Laborintus II*, Andriessen's teacher Berio specified that the three female singers should use microphones, 'without vibrato and avoiding "operatic" voice production'.[16] The close-harmony, vibrato-less singing in parts of this work undoubtedly constitutes an important precedent for the vocal writing in *De Staat*. Earlier in the twentieth century, Hanns Eisler specifically requested that the chorus in *Die Massnahme* should avoid the '"lovely singing" typical of choral societies'. Instead, the singer must aim at 'a very precise, tight, rhythmic kind of singing',

---

15 See the similar statements in Kimberley 1996 and Van Rossum and Smit 1994.
16 Composer's note in score to *Laborintus II*.

presenting his or her notes 'like a report at a mass meeting, i.e. cold, sharp and trenchant'.[17] This 'agitatory' vocal style left its mark on a number of Andriessen's vocal works including *De Staat*, as I discuss further in Chapter 4. Equally important to Andriessen's approach to singing style, though, were the popular vocal ensembles of the 1950s. As a child, Andriessen enjoyed the barbershop crooning of the Four Freshmen, and in 1959 he discovered the music of 'Les Double Six' – who later became the Swingle Singers. Andriessen has commented, 'it's only when I hear four people singing really beautiful chords together that I'm moved to tears.... Nothing is more beautiful' (Van Rossum and Smit 1994, pp. 13–14).

Jazz performance styles appealed, then, as part of a wider concern to escape the instrumental and vocal styles associated with classical music. But Andriessen was interested too in the way that jazz performers cultivated a 'personal sound',[18] one that reflected the individual personality of the musicians – where classical training appeared only to effect a homogenization, even a depersonalization of style. This, of course, was consistent with the democratizing motivation behind the creation of the Orkest De Volharding: its musicians were no longer subservient labour, toiling for other people's benefit, but free individuals able to express their tastes and preferences. It had dramatic consequences for the sound of De Volharding:

> Classical musicians are really a medium. They say, 'You write a B flat, I give you a B flat.' But a colleague, a classically-trained composer, wrote for De Volharding, and after a rehearsal came to me: 'It's completely different to all my former experiences, because when I write a B flat, I don't get back my B flat, I get De Volharding back.' You see the difference? (Andriessen, in Witts 1978, p. 9)

There was a careful balancing act to be performed here. While Andriessen's aspirations for democratic music-making demanded an identification between music and musician, they also placed a premium on equality and solidarity. In his music for De Volharding, the idea of unison became an overriding concern.[19] This meant that the soloistic focus of traditional jazz had to be discarded. There is a parallel here with the 'free jazz' of John Coltrane and Ornette Coleman in the 1960s, which similarly sought to overcome the sharp differentiation between soloist and accompaniment and accord equality to all the musicians. But where Coltrane and Coleman pioneeered the idea of

---

[17] Eisler, in Brecht 1997, p. 233.
[18] On this characteristic of jazz see Kernfeld 1995, p. 169 and Jackson 2002, p. 89.
[19] See the discussion of unison in Ch. 4.

'collective improvisation', Andriessen preferred the more traditional composerly role of setting down exactly what the musicians were to do, albeit following periods of consultation with the musicians of De Volharding. That is not to say that there are no freedoms in these works: *De Volharding* leaves the number of its many repetitions unspecified, in classic minimalist style; *On Jimmy Yancey* allows performers to invent their own boogie licks in a number of places; and *Workers Union* notates approximate register but not precise pitch. But improvisation remained principally a tool for composition rather than an opportunity for performers: 'I do improvise a lot on the piano and I find musical ideas out of playing. Obviously, I first have a certain vision of what kind of piece I would like to write, but then I start to play and improvise. I need the physical contact with the sound' (Andriessen, in Trochimczyk (ed.) 2002, p. 171). In the following chapter, we will see that improvisation played a particularly important role in the composition of *De Staat*.

Instead of making their presence felt through improvisation, the musicians of De Volharding declared their stake in the proceedings through the 'physical investment' (Tra 1978, p. 10) and energy with which they engaged with the music. This was also something that Andriessen associated with jazz: it 'has a musical quality which is common to all folk music and which is almost completely neglected by western art music, that is the "physical" qualities of playing' (Andriessen 1972, p. 131). In this way, collective application replaced individualistic showmanship. The instruction on the front page of the score of *Workers Union* (1975) sums up the approach to performance of the Orkest De Volharding more generally: 'Only in the case that every player plays with such an intention that his part is an essential one, will the work succeed; just as in the political work.'

At one level this was simply a matter of volume. The aggressive loudness of De Volharding – their publicity favoured the word *keihard*, literally meaning 'rock hard', more figuratively 'at full blast'[20] – was at once an expression of the music's protesting, agitprop qualities and the collective commitment of the musicians. It left an unmistakable imprint on much of Andriessen's later music. But the desire for complete performer commitment also lent to his music of the 1970s a kind of hectic strenuousness, as works came to be conceived principally as a set of challenges to the corporate ensemble. *Workers Union* is one of the clearest examples of this attitude. Andriessen describes it as a 'symphonic movement for any loud-sounding group of instruments'. As with Riley's *In C*, the score comprises a single line of music which is used by all the musicians. In contrast to *In C*, however,

---

[20] See e.g. Van Marissing 1973.

Andriessen does not use conventional staff notation: instead, the music is notated on a single line which indicates approximate register only. Musicians are instructed to choose their own notes, with the general requirement that the music should sound 'dissonant, chromatic and often: aggressive'. And where *In C* allows individual musicians to proceed through the score at their own pace, *Workers Union* enforces complete rhythmic unanimity. The result carries echoes of both the unrelieved drive of bebop and the rhythmic precision and exaggerated gestures of 1950s big bands. Kevin Whitehead has proposed a particular kinship with Stan Kenton (Whitehead 1999, pp. 243, 248): this may be heard in the attempts to whip up successive, ever greater waves of manic energy; in the use of extreme registral contrasts; and in the 'vulgar' unpitched slides preceding many notes. Implicit in Whitehead's comparison, though, is a criticism, for Kenton has often been accused of over-inflated bombast, and the same criticism has also been levelled at Andriessen's music – not least *De Staat*, which shares some of the haranguing quality of *Workers Union*. But it was Andriessen's belief at this time that the success of a piece could not be viewed independently of its relation to the musicians who performed it. The score was only half of the equation, a stimulus for what really mattered: the unflagging musical endeavour of the performers. This philosophy of performance continued to inform later works written for other musicians, including *Hoketus* (1977) and *De Staat* itself. In 1978 Andriessen described the difference this attitude made to the end result:

> You could not 'translate' my piece *Hoketus* for the symphony orchestra, because the piece is unbreakably linked to the characteristics and mentality of the musicians who play it. For that piece, an unbelievable amount of power and motivation is requested because that is what that music radiates. You feel how closely these people are involved with this music. It is something from themselves. (In Op de Coul 1979)

Minimalism

As we saw in Chapter 1, American minimalism counterpointed jazz as a second important stimulus for Andriessen at the start of the seventies. The decisive experience was the first recording of Terry Riley's *In C*, which Frederic Rzewski brought to Andriessen's attention in 1970.[21] But Andriessen also made the acquaintance of other music by prominent figures in minimalist composition during 1970 and 1971. He met Steve Reich in Amsterdam in 1971

---

[21] See Ch. 1.

(Trochimczyk (ed.) 2002, p. 20),[22] by which time he had already heard Reich's *Piano Phase* (1967), *Pendulum Music* (1968) and *Four Organs* (1970) (Andriessen 1995b, p. 113; Reich 2002, p. 227).[23] He also heard the recording of Philip Glass's *Music with Changing Parts* (1970) during a trip to New York: this appealed to him because it was 'more radical' than Reich's music (Andriessen 1995b, p. 113).[24] In 1975 Glass toured to the Netherlands with his ensemble, playing *Music with Changing Parts*, *Another Look at Harmony*, and sections of *Music in Twelve Parts*. In an interview given shortly after one of these performances, Andriessen commented that 'Glass radiates a ... luxuriousness that I don't care for – but which I somehow like at the same time.... It does prick the pretensions of the avant-garde' (Andriessen, in Koopmans 1976b, p. 36). As we will see, resonances of music by all three of these composers are frequently encountered, not just in Andriessen's works from the early seventies but in *De Staat* as well.

As important as any of these, though, was the music of Frederic Rzewski himself.[25] Andriessen first met Rzewski in Berlin in 1964. Though American by birth, Rzewski spent much of his time in Europe during the 1960s, where he was a prominent figure in the improvised music scene (Nyman 1999, pp. 128–31). Towards the end of the sixties he also played as a keyboardist in some early performances of the Philip Glass Ensemble (Potter 2000, p. 287), and this experience led to his own music taking a minimalist turn. His *Les Moutons de Panurge* ('The Sheep of Panurge') (1969) comprises a single line of music for any number of musicians, which is accompanied by free improvisation from any number of 'non-musicians'.[26] The notated line is not played straight through, but rather is used to generate repeated melodic cells played by all the musicians in unison; these expand by one note on each occurrence, an additive principle shared with Glass's early works. But Rzewski's piece also has characteristics not found in other early American minimalism. It uses a non-diatonic scale – the white-note scale with flattened A and B – where other early minimalism uses diatonic modes. It is marked

---

[22] Elsewhere Andriessen dates his meeting as '1970 or 71' (Andriessen 1990b, p. 152); Reich, however, dates it to 1972, when his ensemble first performed in the Netherlands (Reich 2002, p. 227).

[23] Reich also suggests that Andriessen encountered *Drumming* (1971) soon after it was written.

[24] Andriessen says that he heard the recording only once, in New York (letter to the author, 13 February 2003).

[25] Andriessen pointed to the importance of Rzewski's music in a letter to the author (13 February 2003).

[26] The complete score is reproduced in Nyman 1999, p. 158.

'sempre *ff*', giving the piece a fierce energy quite distinct from the more contemplative aura created by Glass and Reich. And in instructing the performers to 'never stop or falter ... stay together as long as you can',[27] it provides a direct forerunner to Andriessen's conception of ensemble performance as collective perseverance.

There is no doubt that aspects of minimalism – its rhythmic drive, improvisatory elements, and allusion to popular and non-Western musics – held great appeal for Andriessen in the early seventies, and Rzewski's music suggested that these qualities did not necessarily come at the expense of earthy vigour. Andriessen himself is now often referred to as a 'minimalist' composer, on account of the prominence of repetitive textures in his music. It is a designation he hotly contests. This is partly due to an objection to the term itself: like Reich, he prefers to talk of 'repetitive' music.[28] But it is also due to his conviction that minimalism is only one idiom amongst many to be alluded to in his music; he prefers to see his music as, in fact, 'MAXIMAL music – I am a maximalist!' (in Johnson 1994, p. 758). Even in the most sparely reductive works of the early seventies, other sources than American minimalism could be detected behind his newly economical style. The 'conceptual music' of his friends Dick Raaijmakers and Gilius van Bergeijk was one (see Ch. 1). Their pieces had little in common with the buoyant patterned processes of the Americans, yet were nevertheless 'based on a single idea, on a musical idea, and the result is purely a development of this idea' (Andriessen, in Gronemeyer 1992, p. 54). The 'minimalism' of *Melodie* for recorder and piano (1974), a 25-minute examination of near-unison playing which is 'without repetition but continually the same',[29] is related principally to this kind of focused conceptualism, rather than Reich and Glass. The music of Eisler provided another encouragement for a pared-down style. The insistent march-like iterations and simple ostinati, sparing use of dynamics and lack of phrasing in Eisler's music for *Die Massnahme* set the standard for Andriessen's own approach to 'applied music', and are echoed in works such as *Il Principe* ('The Prince') (1974) and *Workers Union*.

Even in *De Volharding* ('Perseverance') (1972), which Kevin Whitehead has proposed is 'in many ways ... *In C* remade' (Whitehead 1997, p. 6), a number of quite different stylistic influences also make their presence felt.

---

[27] There is an ironic connection with the title here, for 'Panurge's sheep' is a derogatory expression used in France for people who unthinkingly follow their leader.

[28] Letter to the author (13 February 2003).

[29] Andriessen, sleeve note to LP recording of *Melodie* (Attacca Babel 9267–6).

Like *In C*, the piece comprises a succession of small fragments of melodic material, each of which is repeated many times. Rather than provide a single line for all the musicians, Andriessen writes individual parts for the different instruments, but they are frequently close variants of each other and there remains a sense of all the musicians proceeding through the same material at slightly different speeds. The gradually shifting patterns of the opening piano solo – which begins with the two notes that dominate the opening bars of *In C* (E and F above middle C) – helps to establish an authentically minimalist feel. This is bolstered in a lengthy passage in the middle of the piece (beginning at 8'20 on the recording), whose closely registered, gradually shifting melodic patterns could have been lifted direct from Riley's piece. The musicians' leisurely progress through this section at the premiere was sufficiently provocative to stimulate the jeering, whistling and applause that then accompanies the rest of the performance. For a substantial proportion of the large Amsterdam audience, this will have been their first exposure to the rigours of purist minimalism.

And yet significant differences from American models are also apparent from the start. The placing of new material, rather than being left to individual performers' discretion as in *In C*, is carefully controlled by positioning on the playing score and extensive verbal instructions. The modular format of the score consequently resembles the graphical intricacies of Boulez's *Eclat* (one of the original inspirations mentioned by Andriessen (Andriessen 1972, p. 131)) as much as any minimalist precedent. Similarly, while Andriessen does not specify precise numbers of repetitions of the successive modules of material, the musicians are nevertheless periodically marshalled into compulsory noisy unisons, Andriessen's ideological interest in collective unanimity dictating the periodic overriding of Rileyesque individual freedom. The whole is additionally spiced with devices that are more Stravinskian than minimalist: sudden discontinuities that shatter American minimalism's guiding notion of 'music as a gradual process'; registral adventurousness, as at [K] where all the instruments suddenly plunge into the bass (foreshadowing a fundamental gesture of *De Staat*);[30] and, not least, gritty chromatic harmony.

That Andriessen was not prepared unthinkingly to adopt the compositional procedures of the American minimalists was further demonstrated in the tape piece *Il Duce* ('The Duke') (1973). The work is based on a speech by Mussolini; Andriessen's treatment of it, which involved selecting a small portion and repeating it over and over in a way that gradually obscures the original verbal content, strongly resembles the early tape pieces of Steve

---

[30] This happens at 14'47 on the CD.

Reich, particularly *Come Out* (1965) and *It's Gonna Rain* (1966).[31] However, *Il Duce* is intended as something of a riposte to Reich's works. In his article about composing for Brecht's *Die Massnahme*, Andriessen alludes to 'American electronic avant-garde music' in which 'words or sentences are often repeated unendingly. Within the shortest possible time, the listener has forgotten the text and word becomes sound' (Andriessen 1975, p. 439). Andriessen's implication, both in this article and in *Il Duce*, is that such endless repetition should be applied to text only where there is good reason to obscure its meaning; the propaganda of Mussolini is more deserving of this treatment than the black preacher of *It's Gonna Rain* or the beaten black youth in *Come Out*. To ram the point home, Andriessen closes his piece with the grandiose opening strains of Strauss's *Also sprach Zarathustra*.

Andriessen's observation about the aestheticizing tendencies of Reich's early tape pieces – works that by virtue of their source material ought to have been strong political statements – chimed with the growing reservations about minimalism he and his colleagues had as the seventies progressed. Reich's and Glass's preference for performing their music in art galleries once seemed a brave departure from concert-giving convention. But in the light of the Volharding experience, it increasingly seemed to signify merely a continued pandering to the art-consuming bourgeoisie.[32] Equally, the voluptuous tendency in Glass's music brought it dangerously close to the mindlessness (as Andriessen saw it) of commercial pop.

Andriessen's increasingly ambivalent feelings about minimalism find their most powerful expression in *Hoketus* (1977). This piece originated in a special project on 'Minimal music' taught by Andriessen at the Hague Conservatory in early 1976 – while work was still ongoing on *De Staat*. The students taking this course had a wide range of experience: all were studying instruments or composition at the Conservatory, but a number were also rock musicians. Andriessen ranged widely over numerous subjects pertaining to minimalism: classes were held on Reich's *It's Gonna Rain* and *Violin Phase*, Dada, Satie, Cage, kinetic art, Fluxus and Riley's *In C* (Hiu 1993, p. 75). There was, however, some hostility towards the glossiness and apparent banality of American minimal music amongst the students: Reich's music was, in the

---

[31] Andriessen acknowledges the indebtedness in Gronemeyer 1992, p. 55. The technical process of *Il Duce*, which involves the cumulative build-up of the distortion on the original recording, is in fact closer to Alvin Lucier's *I am Sitting in a Room* (1970), but Andriessen's interest in this technique predates Lucier's piece: it is also used in *Zangen van Maldoror*, a little-known tape piece from 1968.

[32] See Reinbert de Leeuw's comments in Koopmans 1976b, p. 35.

words of one student, 'roombotermuziek' (literally, 'buttercream-music')
(ibid.). Andriessen was prepared to acknowledge that minimal music had in
recent years developed an undeniable 'TV advertisement association', but he
wanted to persuade the students that minimalism had originated as 'a rigid [i.e.
strict] and radical' approach to composition (Andriessen, in Whitehead 1999,
p. 245). To do this, he organized a performance of *In C*, and in order to avoid
the hazy smoothness of the original recording the students played it, as
Andriessen later put it, 'BANG BANG BANG BANG BANG' (ibid., p. 246).
Then he set a composition exercise: everyone, including Andriessen himself,
wrote a short 'minimal' study.[33] Andriessen's exercise was to be the basis for
Hoketus. The class, meanwhile, with its odd assortment of instruments
(panpipes, pianos, keyboards, electric guitars and untuned percussion; the rock
association was underlined by the use of heavy amplification) eventually
became the ensemble of the same name.

Andriessen's programme note to *Hoketus* clearly states its intent: the piece
'makes use of certain stylistic devices of minimal art, but at the same time
criticises this style.... The harmonic material is not diatonic but chromatic, and
[the piece] radically abandons the continuous tonal sound-masses
characteristic of most minimal art, including all accompanying cosmic
nonsense.'[34] The title derives from the work's basic principle, namely 'hocket'
– a medieval musical technique whereby consecutive notes in a melody are
distributed between two or more voices.[35] The ensemble is divided into two
equal halves placed on either side of the stage, and these spend most of the
piece hurling chords at each other in rapid alternation. In formal terms, though,
the point of reference is clearly Steve Reich. As in many of Reich's early
pieces, *Hoketus* falls into three main sections (excluding the coda),[36] and each
of these involves the gradual addition of more notes to a repeated rhythmic
pattern. But far from producing a wholly derivative exercise, Andriessen takes
several steps to transform his work into a horrible minimalist mutant. First,
there is the 'loud and earthy' quality of the ensemble itself (Andriessen, in

[33] Henk Borgdorff, conversation with the author. Borgdorff was a member of the
class.

[34] Composer's programme note to *Hoketus* (Muziekgroep Nederland archive).

[35] Hocket is common in the music of Machaut, with which Andriessen had a long
involvement. Machaut's Mass is quoted in *Contra Tempus*, for instance, and
Andriessen wrote an article on Machaut at about the same time: Andriessen 1968b.

[36] In a letter to the author (4 April 2003) Andriessen disagreed with this analysis,
saying that the music is in *four* sections with a coda. This is correct if the insistently
repeated chord immediately preceding the coda is counted as a section in its own right;
I hear it as a transition or introduction to the coda.

Koopmans 1976a), its hard sonority a far cry from the organs and wind of Glass or the tintinnabular tuned percussion of Reich. The sonic contrast is exacerbated by Andriessen's curdled chromatic harmonies; it is only with the tuneful coda that there is any hint of the diatonicism so beloved of the Americans. Then, in place of the even metres favoured by Reich, Andriessen deploys lopsided time signatures (groups of fives and sevens), making it impossible for the listener to lapse into an unthinking 'groove'. Finally, the music also changes metre regularly, so that whatever metric expectations the listener is able to infer are regularly disrupted. (Reich did not use frequently changing metre until *Tehillim* (1981), by which time he had encountered the comparable metric adventurousness of *De Staat*.[37])

Hoketus received its first performance, in a provisional version, at the end of May 1976. The increase in antiphonal and hocketing textures towards the end of *De Staat* doubtless reflects Andriessen's involvement with this project in the later stages of composition of this piece. In other respects, though, the pieces' attitudes to American minimalism are intriguingly different. *De Staat* is, firstly, more 'through-composed', making much use of repetitious textures but (in contrast to both *De Volharding* and *Hoketus*) without resorting to literal repetition marks. It also includes lengthy passages that are entirely faithful to the sound and spirit of American minimalism, including the intoxicating 'continuous tonal sound-masses' that *Hoketus* specifically set out to oppose. These various traits will be discussed in greater detail in the next chapter. They suggest an attitude to minimalism that, while by no means being unconditionally accepting, is warmer than that presented by *Hoketus*, and is thus more representative of the complex, ambivalent stance taken in the works of the seventies as a whole.

Stravinsky

No review can be written about Louis Andriessen without Stravinsky's name cropping up. This is usually intended as a compliment; but as a composer you can be complimented for your good taste too often. (Schönberger 1993, p. 210)

Andriessen has never hidden his passion for the music of Stravinsky. It is a love that has endured the various stylistic and ideological shifts of his compositional career. As he says, 'I was unfaithful to Stravinsky for a period in the '60s.... But I cannot remember a time when I did not love the music of

---

[37] On the possible influence of *De Staat* on Reich, see Andriessen 1990b, p. 152.

Stravinsky' (in Enright 1996, p. 37). This sense of identification has no more prominent testimonial than the large book about Stravinsky that Andriessen wrote in the early 1980s with Elmer Schönberger, entitled *Het Apollonisch Uurwerk* (*The Apollonian Clockwork*). While the book poses as an idiosyncratic documentary and analytical study of Stravinsky's life and works, Andriessen has more recently confirmed what many of the book's readers suspected from the start: 'a lot of that book is about what I did. It's my homage to composing' (Andriessen and Cross 2003, p. 255).

Andriessen's Stravinskian predilections were apparent in his music long before *The Apollonian Clockwork* was published in 1983. The opening bars of his first published work, *Nocturnen*, with their high winds and plucked strings, tense diatonic harmonies and nervous 're-beginnings',[38] could not announce the connection more clearly. Further, more or less undisguised Stravinsky pastiche crops up at regular intervals in Andriessen's oeuvre. *Canzone 3 (Utinam)* for voice and piano (1962), for instance, a setting from the Book of Job, is entirely based upon a combination of triadic walking bass line and chromatic chords in the treble, which Andriessen could have lifted direct from the third movement of the *Symphony of Psalms* (specifically, the passage at [21]). *Souvenirs d'enfance*, as well as borrowing the subtitle of Stravinsky's *Trois petites chansons* ('Souvenirs de mon enfance'), includes a piece consisting entirely of excerpts from Stravinsky's works. *Anachronie II* (1969) for oboe and chamber orchestra veers queasily between a dreamy film-music style, pointillist avant-gardism and unmistakable allusions to the best-known of all twentieth-century 'recompositions', Stravinsky's *Pulcinella*. Chronologically closer to *De Staat* is the *Symphonies of the Netherlands* for wind band (1974), whose fresh woodwind ostinati and ebullient horns sound like minimalist takes on *Petrushka* and the *Four Norwegian Moods*. And in the same year that *De Staat* was premiered, Andriessen was working with the theatre group Baal on the music-theatre piece *Matthew Passion*: this time it is the neo-Baroque idiom of *Dumbarton Oaks* that rears its head on a number of occasions.

It would seem from these examples that in general it is the more refined neoclassical style of Stravinsky's middle age that is most important to Andriessen. But this would be to overlook the impact of *The Rite of Spring*'s aggressive primitivism on many of his works. Andriessen calls *The Rite* 'the most important historical and revolutionary piece for the next two hundred years' (Andriessen and Thomas 1994, p. 139), and its influence is felt not least

---

[38] On the Stravinskian 'technique of recurrent beginnings' see Trochimczyk (ed.) 2002, pp. 93, 148.

in *De Staat*. The appeal of Stravinsky's music for Andriessen is partly that it embraces both controlled formalism *and* 'passion and carnality' – a combination he admires in other artists too (Andriessen 1995a, p. 72).[39] And in both the 'Russian' and the neoclassical works, Stravinsky espouses what Andriessen calls an 'anti-hierarchical' outlook, one that is prepared to reference and incorporate popular musical sources that are more usually excluded from progressive musics (Andriessen and Cross 2003, p. 252).

As for more specific, technical parallels between the two composers' styles, they are not hard to identify.[40] It was undoubtedly congenial to Andriessen, for instance, that his politically motivated avoidance (after 1969) of string instruments – and especially violins – was consistent with well-known examples in the Stravinsky oeuvre such as the *Symphonies of Wind Instruments*, the Concerto for Piano and Winds, and the *Symphony of Psalms* (which replaced violins and violas with two grand pianos). Andriessen's approach to orchestration also reflects Stravinsky's preference for treating texture and timbre as servants to compositional structure, rather than compositional domains in their own right:

> I think of harmony, melody and rhythm as the main parameters of music.... All that whining about textural sonorous fields and special instrumental effects bores me. Instrumentation must correspond to the structure of the music. You'll never hear a flute playing a snatch of a tune in my music. Once it starts its story, it finishes it.[41]

The Rite's rhythmic innovations, meanwhile, are especially apparent in the quirky patterns of *Hoketus* and a number of the harmonically murkier passages of *De Staat* (where asymmetrical accentuation provides the principal structuring force – see for instance bb. 322–57). Elsewhere, though, Andriessen's tendency to conceive of minimalist repetition in terms of toiling endeavour limits the parallels: *De Volharding* and *Workers Union* connote the heavy grind of proletarian struggle as much as the buoyant dance of Nijinsky or Balanchine.

In fact, Andriessen has argued that the real significance of *The Rite* resides

---

[39] Andriessen is here talking about Peter Greenaway. There is a similar comment, this time about the writer Louis Ferron, in Andriessen 1976, p. 58.

[40] Jonathan Cross gives an evaluation of the impact of Stravinsky on Andriessen's music in Cross 1998.

[41] Andriessen, in 'Louis Andriessen: Biographical data', <http://www.donemus.nl/en/composers/andriessen_louis/biografie.html>, accessed 21 July 2001. This web page no longer exists, and at the time of writing the short interview it contained had not been transplanted to the new Muziekgroep Nederland website.

not in its approach to rhythm but in its harmony (Andriessen and Cross 2003, p. 254). Stravinsky's fondness, in this and other early works, for juxtaposing contrasting areas of relatively static harmony is particularly germane to Andriessen's works of the seventies. The brief *Hymne to the Memory of Darius Milhaud* (1974), which was written for De Volharding and later orchestrated (Andriessen's one modest concession to the orchestra in the 1970s), serves as a good example (see Ex. 2.1). The 'magical combination of diatonic melodic material and chromatic harmonic material' that Andriessen sees as 'the crux' of *The Rite* (ibid.) is faithfully reproduced in the *Hymne*, and the false relations and bitonal tinge characterizing many of the chords are

Ex. 2.1   Excerpt (sections [A]–[C]) of *Hymne to the Memory of Darius Milhaud* (piano reduction)

consistent with the principles of Stravinsky's 'pandiatonicism' as outlined in
The Apollonian Clockwork (Andriessen and Schönberger 1989, pp. 55–61).
(They also pay homage to Milhaud's *La Création du monde*, and indeed
Andriessen sees the work as reflecting 'Milhaud's interpretation of
Stravinsky' as much as Stravinsky himself.[42]) The larger design of the piece is
also unmistakably Stravinskian. Three of the work's four distinct sections
comprise simply a few triadic or thirds-based chords in treble and bass,
repeated and permutated so that different chords collide. Stravinsky deployed
similarly restricted means in a number of pieces written in the years following
The Rite. Sometimes, compositional options are shrunk to the extent that the
music is 'virtually reduced to the level of wind-up toy automata' (Taruskin
1996, p. 1450). In Stravinsky's *Valse pour les enfants* for piano (*c*.1916), for
instance, the 'vamping' left hand obstinately alternates only two chords, just
as the lower instruments do within each section of the *Hymne*.[43] Closer to the
Hymne in mood, though, is the third of Stravinsky's Three Pieces for String
Quartet, whose chromatic chorale textures are generated in the same
permutational way. In the *Hymne* Andriessen appears to have combined the
generative technique of the quartet piece with the registral spacing (with its
characteristic tenths) and more spacious timing of the closing chorale of
Stravinsky's own memorial work, the *Symphonies of Wind Instruments*.

On the surface, the furious energy of *De Staat* is far removed from these
poised models. But there remains a characteristically Stravinskian concern for
harmonic staticity and inner permutation over decisive movement. And if the
biting dissonances of the later piece derive from the chromaticism of *The Rite*
rather than the more triad-based works that follow, they nevertheless remain
recognizably connected to the scales and formations familiar in tonality. The
next chapter will examine these in some depth.

The *Hymne*'s harmonic and textural resemblances to Stravinsky are
reinforced by the lack of dynamic nuance or orchestrational complexity: the
music achieves a strongly ritualistic quality without forgoing the roughness
so central to the Volharding aesthetic. A similar monumental staticity affects *Il
Principe* (1974), and in this piece the Stravinskian principle of block form is
more rudely apparent – as it had already been in a number of Andriessen's
works from the sixties. The work is scored for two choirs: the first chants
extracts from Machiavelli's *The Prince* in rhythmic unison, doubled by a
wind-dominated instrumental ensemble; the other is a small vocal group that
interrupts the large choir with extracts from Gesualdo's Sixth Book of

---

[42] Letter to the author (4 April 2003).
[43] The *Valse* is reproduced in Taruskin 1996, p. 1450.

Madrigals.[44] Over a century separates Andriessen's two Renaissance sources, but there are nevertheless connections to be drawn between them: Gesualdo himself was a hereditary prince, and the work of both examines death, destruction and cruelty (Desmedt 1988, p. 183) – commonalities of theme that are exploited in the small choir's 'comments' on the Machiavelli text. However, the dramatically contrasting musical styles of the two choirs establishes a tense opposition between writer and composer, one that is quite in keeping with the strategies of juxtaposition in many of Stravinsky's early works (see Cone 1962).

The inclusion of the Gesualdo extracts may itself be an act of homage to Stravinsky, whose passion for the Italian composer culminated in the orchestral *Monumentum pro Gesualdo* (1960).[45] The chanting style of many of Stravinsky's choral works is clearly evoked in *Il Principe*. In his Russian settings of the Pater Noster and Credo, and the Credo of his Mass, Stravinsky adopts the homophonic style of Russian Orthodox chant, with simple syllabic rhythms clearly projecting the text. His *Threni* and *Requiem Canticles* take the idea a stage further, with music for a speaking chorus. In *Il Principe* the Machiavelli text is similarly delivered in a relentless homophonic chant, which falls somewhere between the euphonious Orthodox style and rhythmic speech: pitches are notated, but the narrow register and rapid rhythms mean that it sounds highly speech-like. (The influence of the speech-song style that Andriessen developed in 1972 for Brecht's *Die Massnahme* is important here too; see Ch. 4.) The spoken chant sections of *Threni* seem to have left their mark on the instrumental writing in *Il Principe*, which, besides doubling the principal choir, is characterized by sporadic, strongly accented iambic interjections; *Threni*'s chanting chorus is punctuated by similar dyadic figures.[46] Both the choral and instrumental writing here strongly foreshadows the central choral section of *De Staat*; it is not without reason that Andriessen later referred to *Il Principe* as his 'klein Staatje' ('little *Staat*') (Desmedt 1988, p. 188).

There are, then, numerous ways in which Stravinsky's music affected Andriessen's during the 1970s. But arguably more important than any of those so far mentioned was the example set by Stravinsky with regard to matters of expression and stylistic reference. Andriessen has often declared: 'I'm a

---

[44] The texts are reproduced in Appendix C.

[45] Andriessen, like Stravinsky, took a quasi-scholarly interest in Gesualdo's music: see Andriessen 1968a.

[46] Andriessen is an enthusiastic advocate of Stravinsky's *Threni*; see his choice of 'Desert Island Discs' in *Het Parool*, 30 September 1997, p. 16.

classicist and not a romantic' (Potter 1981, p. 17), an orientation that, as *The Apollonian Clockwork* reminds us, he shares with Stravinsky. Andriessen and Schönberger offer the following definitions:

> Classical in this instance means music in which the composer creates only the form 'but leaves the finding of some content in this form to "the listener's powers of imagination"'. '... The listener, too, must autonomously collaborate at fulfillment.' Romanticism imputes to music 'concrete content, condemning the listener to passivity'. 'Where music makes use of such intensified means that it despotically sweeps the listener under its spell and robs him of his own power of imagination, it ceases to be music.' (Andriessen and Schönberger 1989, p. 100)[47]

Andriessen and Schönberger's characterization of Stravinsky is based on his well-known statements about expression in music. His contention that 'music is, by its very nature, essentially powerless to express anything at all' announced the primacy of form and method over representation – especially the representation of the composer's emotions (Stravinsky 1962, p. 53).[48] For the young Andriessen, Stravinsky's dictum promised a welcome release from the emotional self-absorption of the late Romantics and their twentieth-century heirs: already in 1968 Andriessen was celebrating the idea of a composer for whom 'sentiment can be the motor of composition but never the intended aim' (Andriessen 1968b, p. 86). Romantic music, by contrast, was bedevilled by 'artistic narcissism' (Andriessen 1966, p. 53). Mahler thus formed the opposite pole to Stravinsky:

> Stravinsky displays objects, makes gestures. Mahler gives voice to himself. Stravinsky the person is hidden behind the artwork. Mahler reveals himself as a *Mensch*, typically romantic: just listen to how deeply I suffer, listen to how happy I am. That type of composer means nothing to me. (Andriessen, in Van Rossum and Smit 1994, p. 11)

In holding these views, Andriessen does not wish to deny that music can cause an emotional response: he admits to being 'moved to tears by Stravinsky's music', for instance, and in his discussions with Maja Trochimczyk he makes frequent reference to the melancholy, joy and other emotions caused by

---

[47] The citations are drawn from Albert Roussel, Arthur Berger and Friedrich Blume.

[48] See also Stravinsky 1947, p. 77. The *Autobiography* and the *Poetics of Music* were both substantially ghost-written (see Michael Oliver, *Igor Stravinsky* (London: Phaidon, 1995), 107), but they remain central to our reception of Stravinsky's music.

music.[49] But for Andriessen this reaction cannot be taken as any indication of the composer's emotional state: rather, it is a simple effect of the musical material itself. In his words, 'the product of what we do is far more important than we ourselves are. And that is probably what you call my anti-romanticism' (Andriessen, in Enright 1996, p. 34).

Thus Andriessen conceives of himself as the 'homo faber' described by Stravinsky in his *Poetics* (Stravinsky 1947, pp. 50–53): someone who discovers and invents, rather than introspectively exploring the depths of his or her own psyche. 'Work, making something', Andriessen proposed shortly before the premiere of *De Staat*, is a necessary antidote to current trends of 'self-discovery' and the preoccupation with self-image encouraged by consumer society (Andriessen, in Koopmans 1976a). At one level this attitude is simply another kind of twentieth-century formalism – the desire for a detached, almost scientific objectivity, consistent with Stravinsky's reductive view of music as the art of sound and time (see Stravinsky 1947, p. 27), or the pure abstraction advocated by Andriessen's beloved Mondrian. And indeed Andriessen has long demonstrated a formalist concern for proportional calculation and elements of pre-composition, as we will see in Chapter 3. His unapologetic reference to beauty in music sometimes confirms the impression of an adherence to an essentially Kantian idea of 'purposeless' formalism.[50]

But in fact, Andriessen draws consequences from his 'classicist' stance that are far removed from the impersonal abstraction it might seem to imply. For by 'disappearing behind the music',[51] the composer is freed from the obligation to embody his or her unique psychology in musical form, and can instead adopt a more flexible relation to existing musical materials, a stance potentially completely at odds with the autonomy claimed by much formalist art. As the Romantic's insistence on originality is relaxed, so the composer may appropriate other musics as he or she sees fit. In his *Poetics* Stravinsky himself made clear that he had little time for the view of the living artist as 'a monster of originality', for whom 'the use of already employed materials and of established forms is usually forbidden' (Stravinsky 1947, p. 73). As Andriessen and Schönberger observe, for Stravinsky, the realizations 'that music is about other music' and that it 'is not primarily suited to express personal emotions' went hand in hand: new music thus 'implies the existence

---

[49] See René T'Sas, 'Andriessen en Schönberger over Strawinsky', *HN-magazine*, 25 June 1983, p. 28; and Andriessen, in Trochimczyk (ed.) 2002, pp. 8–10, 173.

[50] See for instance his description of parts of *De Tijd* in Andriessen and Schönberger 1981, p. 10; or of Ravel's music in Andriessen 1996a, p. 99.

[51] Andriessen, in 'Louis Andriessen: Biographical data'. See above, n. 41.

of other music' (Andriessen and Schönberger 1989, p. 100). Of course, there remain a number of different attitudes a composer may take to existing music, and, as I discuss in the central section of Chapter 4, Andriessen has explored several of these. I suggest there that *De Staat*'s relation to the minimalist styles it incorporates, in particular, deserves careful attention, for it is not immediately clear whether the references are intended as critique or celebration.

There is another apparent paradox in Andriessen's description of himself as a 'classicist'. This description, like the title of Andriessen's and Schönberger's book, seems to give the Apollonian perspective, 'in which form and method take precedence over raw expressive individuality' (Walsh 1993, p. 25), ascendancy.[52] Yet Andriessen's music is often indubitably 'rawly individual', possessing a spontaneity and abandon seemingly completely opposed to the polite order of Stravinsky's classicism. And nowhere is the Dionysian element more rampant than in *De Staat*, with its wild energy and moments of unbridled anger, joy and earnest passion. Despite his suspicion of composers who publicly parade their psychological lives, Andriessen has never pretended to be detached from the world of emotions,[53] and it is not difficult to hear a similar openness and susceptibility to feeling in his music. Part of the appeal of a piece like *De Staat* lies in the recognizable connections it strikes up with conventions for the musical representation of emotional states.

Andriessen has sometimes sought to extricate himself from this seeming contradiction by explaining the expressive content of his music in terms of the referencing of other music: that is to say, the emotion is not directly expressed, but 'quoted', as it were, at one remove:

> I don't want you to be swept away by my music. It must *seem* that you get swept away. Mahler is genuinely overwhelming, but music should be *about* overwhelmingness.... Your emotions and passions function as an energy, as a motor to create music, but you cannot compose them directly into music.... I'm the first to admit that music is, in an exceptionally strong way, about passion. It does not express passion but is a *photo* of passion. (In Koning and Jansen 1981, p. 14)

Arguably, though, such tortuous distinctions between actual and represented emotions are not necessary in order to remain faithful to the principles of

---

[52] Discussions of the 'Apollonian' and the 'Dionysian' in music are usually rooted in the opposition described by Nietzsche in *The Birth of Tragedy*. For Nietzsche, Apollonian and Dionysian represented contrary impulses in artistic creation, towards order and artifice on the one hand, and intoxication and reality on the other.

[53] See for instance his descriptions of joy and love in Trochimczyk (ed.) 2002, p. 229 and Andriessen 1996a, p. 72.

Stravinskian classicism. In his *Poetics*, Stravinsky notes André Gide's aphorism that 'classical works are beautiful only by virtue of their subjugated romanticism', and he uses Tchaikovsky and Weber as examples of composers who do not expunge the passion or ardour to which they are naturally inclined, but contain (or 'subjugate') it through use of a coolly rational form (Stravinsky 1947, pp. 79–80). Viewed in this way, the Apollonian is not opposed to the Dionysian, but its necessary corollary:[54]

> What is important for the lucid ordering of the work – for its crystallization – is that all the Dionysian elements which set the imagination of the artist in motion and make the life-sap rise must be properly subjugated before they intoxicate us, and must finally be made to submit to the law: Apollo demands it. (Ibid., pp. 80–81)

It was noted earlier that Andriessen finds this kind of combination of 'coldness and warmth, of involvement and distance' (Andriessen 1976, p. 58) – in Stravinsky's terms, the Dionysian kept in check by the Apollonian – appealing in other artists. Just such a 'subjugated romanticism' is surely fundamental to *De Staat*, something that is clearer to see if we conceive of romanticism, not exclusively in terms of the tortured narratives of Wagner, Mahler and Schoenberg, but as denoting the more general impulse to convey the 'irrational' through 'intensified means'.[55] This is the impulse that Stravinsky detected in Tchaikovsky; while it is perhaps less evident in Stravinsky's neoclassical works of the twenties and thirties, it may readily be heard in *The Rite of Spring*. And as with these other, earlier cases, *De Staat*'s engagement with human emotional and physical states is prevented from degenerating into a dubious attempt to mimic human psychology by the severe constraints of pure form. These constraints take two principal guises in *De Staat*: a strict proportional scheme determining aspects of the work's montage-like juxtapositions,[56] and a preoccupation with tetrachords (harmonies of four notes). As we will see in the following chapter, if *De Staat* has one pre-eminent characteristic, it is the tension that exists between these formal obligations and Andriessen's passionate, communicative musical instinct.

---

[54] Arnold Whittall makes a similar point in relation to Stravinsky and Andriessen in Whittall 2001, p. 10.

[55] The quotations here are taken from Stravinsky 1947, p. 79 and Andriessen and Schönberger 1989, p. 100.

[56] Andriessen has described montage technique as 'essentially anti-Romantic'; Andriessen and Terreehorst 1981.

Chapter 3

De Staat: The Music

With three opening gestures, *De Staat* starkly announces its basic terms of operation. First: two oboes and two cors anglais, impassively traversing back and forth across a severely restricted pitch terrain. The music's timbre, harmony and ritualistic coolness connote a primitivistic notion of ancient Greece. Second: four trombones (later joined by four horns), grinding out claustrophobic chromatic chords in antithesis to the white-note sonorities of the oboes. Accents, crescendos and a number of fitful, foiled ascents build an increasing tension. Third: the puncturing release of a single bass guitar note, triggering buoyant minimalist textures and sweet, major-key harmonies – one of the great moments in twentieth-century music. The 'vulgar' connotations of electric guitars, regular repetition and bass-oriented harmony are here irresistibly yoked together with words from Plato's *Republic*, sung (in the original ancient Greek) in brazen unison by four microphoned female voices.

The remainder of *De Staat* reverberates with the bold sounds and juxtapositions presented in these opening minutes. Three choral sections, setting extracts of Plato's discussion of the social function of music and arranged symmetrically towards the beginning, middle and end of the work, provide the principal landmarks.[1] Around and between these, Andriessen's distinctive instrumental ensemble – four each of oboes (doubling cor anglais), trumpets, horns, trombones and violas, plus two electric guitars, electric bass, two harps and two pianos, placed (in classic modernist manner) in a 'ritualistic' symmetrical stage layout – is alternately exploited for its clear-cut instrumental contrasts and brought together in fearsome tuttis. The abrupt contrasts of the opening – not least, the contrast of tonal and non-tonal, the search for 'solutions' to which Andriessen regarded as 'the most important issue in contemporary music' (Andriessen and Schönberger 1981, p. 8) – indicate the principle by which the whole work will proceed. Thus *De Staat* embraces both the dreadful harmonic impasse that follows the central choral section (a snarlingly chromatic, eight-note chord, repeatedly uncoiled and retracted by the whole ensemble for almost four minutes) and the patient,

---

[1] A translation of these extracts is contained in Appendix A.

majestic unfolding of the complete diatonic scale immediately prior to the final choral entry. Andriessen's navigation of such contrasts completely eschews gradual transition, but it also seeks to maintain an unflinching energy and drive across the entirety of its 35-minute span. The work's diverse contents are given some measure of common purpose by a rarely relenting fortissimo dynamic, and by a predominance of unison or homorhythmic textures.

These are some of the things a listener will perceive on first hearing *De Staat*. How far beyond this can, or should, a commentary on the music of *De Staat* go? Most listeners will also be aware of a certain coarseness of design, and moments of disjunction or aporia where the music's continuation lacks logic or persuasiveness. *De Staat* is not an unambiguously unified or coherent work; indeed, its formal 'rudeness' constitutes part of its appeal.[2] It would be unfortunate if the synthesizing tendencies of a rigorous analysis were to be allowed to smooth over this characteristic. More generally, there are reasons for viewing the piece as intrinsically anti-aesthetic – that is to say, as intentionally at odds with the value systems that ordinarily underpin assessments of the functioning of musical works. Andriessen's summary of the intention behind his music for De Volharding, namely that it should at all costs avoid being 'frumpy, wispy, artificial, finicky or aesthetic' (De Beer 1985, p. 26), arguably applies as strongly to *De Staat*. If this is correct – and it is an idea that I pursue further in Chapter 4 – then a detailed evaluation of compositional structure will risk constant friction with the spirit of the piece.

In any case, it will be clear from the foregoing chapters that any account of Andriessen's music that contents itself with a structural appraisal – a mapping of formal design, of harmonic and rhythmic elements, or of textural strategies – will fall well short of grasping its significance or meaning. Andriessen's music is integrally bound up with the politics of late twentieth-century musical performance, with a critical view of contemporary culture and society, and with the diverse musical repertoires to which it makes explicit and frequent reference. This is particularly true of the music of the 1970s, when Andriessen's political convictions steered him away from the abstraction of avant-garde compositional styles and cemented a conviction in the social embeddedness of all musical activity. While *De Staat*, with its grandiose scale and more challenging musical idiom, may signal a retreat from the wholehearted cultural involvement that characterized his Volharding work, its political text and programme, its frequently improvisatory abandon, and its

---

[2] Andriessen views 'rudeness', or an 'uncivilized' element, as a characteristic feature of Dutch music and culture; see Trochimczyk (ed.) 2002, p. 8.

sheer, raw sonic splendour risk making analytical dissections of form and harmony seem an academic irrelevance.

It is, nevertheless, to such a discussion that this chapter is devoted. For all that Andriessen has refused, since the early seventies, to take sanctuary in the cosy realm of 'pure music', he retains a strong interest in the qualities and potential of musical material. Indeed, his 'classicist' standpoint (described in Ch. 2), with its insistence that musical materials are about their own properties and not the expressive state of the composer, positively legitimates a focus on music's nuts and bolts. For Andriessen, the workings of musical form and content have their own intrinsic satisfactions and appeal, and this is abundantly clear both from his writings about music and from his own compositions. In the case of *De Staat*, while much was arrived at through improvisation and intuition, formal pre-planning – specifically, a carefully calculated proportional plan, and an interest in the play of various tetrachords (that is, groups of four notes) – also played an important role. These elements of pre-compositional design are outlined in the first section of this chapter, and they provide the point of departure for a more detailed assessment of other formal characteristics of the work. Rather than build a single, unitary account, this assessment offers a number of different angles on the music. In the second section, I identify a small repertoire of types of material that account for the bulk of *De Staat*, and trace their various instantiations throughout the piece. Each type of material can be seen as reflecting an aspect of Andriessen's voracious engagement with other musics. The third and fourth sections examine the harmony of *De Staat* from different perspectives.[3] In the extracts from the *Republic* set by Andriessen, Plato dwells on the question of modes, and this has encouraged a number of commentators to seek parallels in Andriessen's own deployment of diatonic harmony. In the third section of this chapter, I do the same, partly because a modal approach is in many respects appropriate to the work's musical language, but also in order to put right some misunderstandings in existing discussions. This leads to an assessment, in the final section, of the work's relation to tonality. Andriessen is scrupulously careful throughout *De Staat* to avoid any straightforward evocation of traditional tonal practice, but tonality nevertheless plays an important role in the piece. Indeed, the work's distinctive appropriation of tonal elements is one of its most fascinating and influential features.

It is in these last two sections that my discussion departs furthest from

---

[3] Other elements of the work not dealt with in detail in my account – such as rhythm and texture – have received some attention in other analytical studies of *De Staat*: see Everett, forthcoming; Rupprecht 1997.

Andriessen's conscious concerns. This brings a particular risk of the inappropriately 'aesthetic' viewpoint mentioned earlier. But it also presents the opportunity for a fuller recognition of the distinctive friction that exists between the piece's politicized rejection of the organizational finesse of both nineteenth-century 'bourgeois' music and the avant-garde, and its contrary tendencies towards loose-limbed control and balance. An important role is played, too, by the complementary discussion in the following chapter. *De Staat* is clearly as much 'about' the issues raised by Plato's *Republic*, or a particular philosophy of performance, as it is 'about' a certain approach to harmony, for instance. These and other interpretations that reach 'beyond the notes' are considered at some length in Chapter 4. In fact, the discussion there should be considered an extension of the present chapter; one, moreover, that deals more thoroughly with certain parts of the work that are here mentioned only in passing. Nevertheless, to disregard the work's 'purely musical' attributes is to risk missing one of the principal reasons for *De Staat*'s enduring success. As with so much of Andriessen's music, beneath the apparent informality and lack of refinement lies a more complex, subtle play of elements that help give the music its particular power and appeal.

Proportions and Tetrachords

In his conversations with Maja Trochimczyk, Andriessen describes his pre-compositional planning for *De Staat*:

> In *De Staat* nothing much was fixed except that it should have something to do with four-part chords. To make things *easier* for myself, then I planned the form – where the choruses were to come in, the proportions, timing, and so on. Apart from that, I wrote the piece completely freely, by playing and improvising. In my opinion you can hear that, too. (In Trochimczyk (ed.) 2002, p. 126)

It is clear from this description that much of *De Staat* was generated spontaneously, without a great deal of premeditation. Nevertheless, an initial formal plan helped to ensure that the broad shape of the work remained balanced and satisfying. This sort of preliminary formal planning appears to be a regular practice for Andriessen: 'I always make this kind of drawing before I begin to work on an important piece' (Andriessen 1990a, p. 102). Specifically, he is often concerned to establish a work's durational proportions, a reflection of his belief that 'music is an art of proportions' (Andriessen, in Trochimczyk (ed.) 2002, p. 149). As early as *Contra Tempus* (1968) he determined quite precisely his formal proportions in advance (the work's sections form the ratio 6:4:5:8:7). But similar schemes also prevail in more recent works, which in other respects take a much more relaxed approach to musical design. The three parts of the *Trilogy of the Last Day* (1997), for instance, are proportionally related (9:6:4) (Andriessen 2001), as are the scenes of *Writing to Vermeer* (1999) – the proportions in this case deriving from music by John Cage (Andriessen 2000, p. 316). *Hadewijch* (1989) takes its formal proportions not from another composer, but from the floor plan of Reims Cathedral (Trochimczyk (ed.) 2002, pp. 198–99). Perhaps most famously, the point of departure for *De Stijl* (1985) was a set of proportions exactingly derived from a painting by Mondrian; in this case, the proportional scheme determined not just internal section lengths but orchestration as well (De Beer 1985, pp. 28–29). When it comes to devising the detail of the music, Andriessen's attitude to his formal schemes is characteristically flexible; the final proportions of *De Stijl* differed significantly from the original scheme. The overriding principle is that 'It must sound good, whatever happens. The piece has an overall strictness, but the details often demand an intuitive solution.... As long as I can always fall back on the strict scheme, that's the way I like it' (Andriessen, ibid., p. 30).

Andriessen's formal plan for *De Staat* established certain basic properties of the work.[4] First, the overall length of the piece: this was fixed at 40 minutes in the original sketch, and Andriessen's plan includes calculations of how many bars would be required at a certain crotchet speed in order to yield the desired length. Second, the positioning of the three choral passages: these are placed roughly symmetrically, with two shorter passages towards the beginning and end of the work respectively, and a much larger section near the middle. Andriessen conceives of the choral sections as 'caryatids ... on which the orchestral piece rests' (in Reichenfeld 1976). Third, the broad formal proportions of the work: Andriessen's plan situates the start of the central choral section precisely halfway through the work, and determines the length of each of the surrounding sections to enhance the rough symmetry of the positioning of the choral parts. The original proportion scheme was as follows:

---

[4] The formal plan is contained in the surviving sketches for the work, which remain in the possession of the composer. I am grateful to Yayoi Uno Everett for sending me her copy of the sketches and to Louis Andriessen for permitting this. The sketches include the formal plan under discussion here; a number of pages of calculations of the estimated lengths of different sections of the work; two pages of notes on Greek modes and instruments (derived from the account by Arnold van Akkeren that appears with the original LP recording); a continuity sketch, mostly in piano score (missing the section from bb. 275–408); and some pages of rejected material. Also included is a typescript of the Plato text in transliterated Greek with annotations of the spoken metre.

0'–3'	[introduction]	3'
3'–5'	CHOIR I	2'
5'–20'	[instrumental]	15'
20'–25'	CHOIR II	5'
25'–35'	[instrumental]	10'
35'–37'	CHOIR III	2'
37'–40'	[conclusion]	3'

The central choral section ended up longer than originally planned, and the final choral section and concluding instrumental section were shorter, but the finished work still clearly bears the imprint of the original design.

Andriessen's description of the process of composing *De Staat* gives the impression that, having established the basic outlines of the piece, he then set about generating material in a largely unplanned manner in order to fill this basic mould. The continuity sketches confirm this impression. In a number of places, he appears to have made a note of the estimated elapsed duration in mid-composition – as if to gauge, 'on the hoof' as it were, how much more material was needed before arriving at the next large-scale formal landmark. Several compositional 'dead ends' in the continuity sketch, where he embarked on a new section only to abandon it mid-flow, further attest to this basically improvisatory approach. The intention appears to have been to preserve the spontaneity of the moment-to-moment invention while still keeping an eye on the proportional demands of the larger formal structure within which he was operating.

An added stimulus to Andriessen's moment-to-moment invention was provided by his decision to give a prominent role to tetrachords. As he makes clear in Chapter 5, this was directly prompted by the Plato text. Tetrachords formed the basis of ancient Greek melody. The Greek tetrachord comprised four notes spanning the interval of a fourth (or 'diatessaron'); the precise positioning of the two inner notes in a given tetrachord was determined partly by the mode of a composition, and partly by the particular tuning, or 'genus', adopted in performance (West 1992, pp. 160–62). That Andriessen's approach to tetrachords departs entirely from this model can clearly be seen by reference to Ex. 3.1, which gives a comprehensive harmonic summary of *De Staat*. (This example may be used as a guide for much of the discussion in this chapter.) In keeping with his general attitude to the generation of material, his handling of tetrachords seems to have been informal and intuitive rather than rigorously systematic. Andriessen ignores the Greek requirement to confine tetrachords to the diatessaron, and deploys four-note collections vertically (as chords) as well as horizontally. In other words, his approach is consistent with that of twentieth-century theory, in which a tetrachord comprises simply a set of four pitch-classes.[5] Many of the four-note chords in the work appear to be dictated principally by the improvisatory play of four fingers (or three fingers and a thumb) at the keyboard. The clustered tetrachords dominating the music between bars 239 and 275,[6] for instance, serve, in essence, as 'colour' – providing harmonic thickening to a melodic line rather than constituting structural harmonic entities in their own right. There is ambiguity, too, about which of the work's harmonies count as tetrachords. According to Andriessen, tetrachords may be identified within larger harmonies even when they are not clearly singled out as four-note groups: thus for Andriessen the first four notes of the unison melody at bar 275 comprise the 'Indonesian' tetrachord, even though a fifth pitch is quickly added;[7] and the five-note chord at bar 556 is a tetrachord plus a 'good bass note'.[8]

Factors such as these suggest there is little to be gained by attempting an exhaustive examination of the work's tetrachordal harmonies. Nevertheless, there are three recurrent tetrachords whose role is clearly significant and worth particular mention. Their various appearances are detailed in Table 3.1. The first of these (heard at the very beginning of the work) adheres to the same pitches on each appearance, although the registral configuration changes. The second and third, in contrast, are frequently transposed but retain their original intervallic shape. In addition to the element of continuity provided by the individual appearances of these tetrachords, there is an element of interconnectedness between them. The first and second, initially kept quite distinct, are fused in the five-note harmony at bar 442 – a long passage that offers a temporary synthesis before the rude interruption at bar 492. The third, meanwhile, though enjoying only brief appearances in comparison to the others, nevertheless has a wider involvement in the work by virtue of the fact that it is a rearranged (and transposed) version of the first. (B–C–E–F transposed down a tone results in A–B♭–D–E♭.) Yayoi Uno Everett has also pointed to the fact that the second tetrachord (at b. 105), if inverted, produces the

---

[5] See the second definition of 'Tetrachord' given in *New Grove II*, vol. 25, p. 318.

[6] Bar numbers are included in the widely available Boosey and Hawkes score, but not in the original Donemus edition of the score. Appendix B provides cross-references between bar numbers and rehearsal numbers in order to assist those who have access only to the earlier edition.

[7] Andriessen describes this tetrachord as 'Indonesian' in Ch. 5. The reason for the label is discussed later in this chapter.

[8] Letter to the author (13 February 2003). Els Desmedt's analysis of the tetrachordal structure of *De Staat* also singles out groups of four notes from larger harmonic patterns; see Desmedt 1988, pp. 204–21.

Ex. 3.1   Harmonic summary of *De Staat*

Note: (1) bb. 68–104: squiggly lines indicate all chromatic pitches between outer notes; ellipsis indicates individual chords omitted; (2) b. 105 and *passim*: 8 = bass note doubled at the lower octave; (3) bb. 275–321, 499–515, 523–33 and 840–66: lower octave doublings omitted; (4) b. 580 and *passim*: bracket indicates all notes included in harmony.

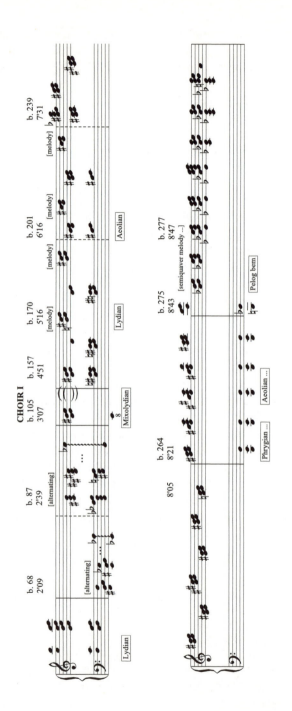

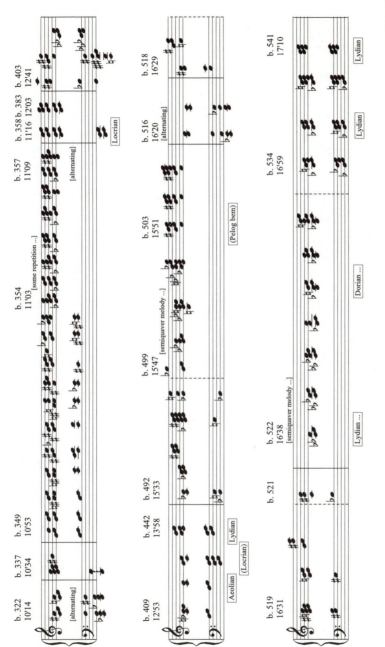

continued

Ex. 3.1 *continued*

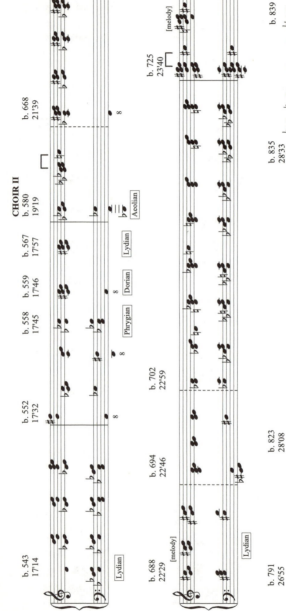

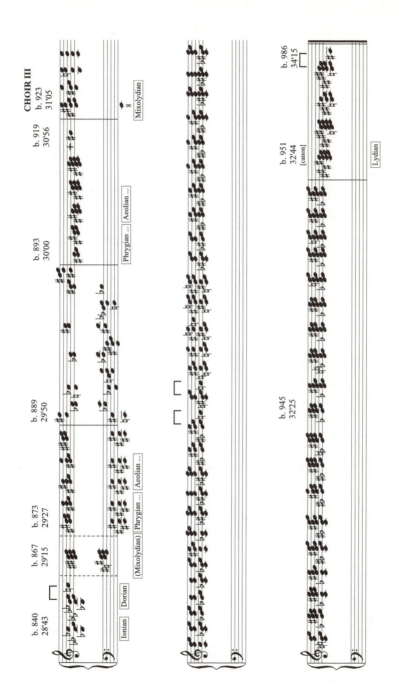

Table 3.1   Recurrent tetrachords in *De Staat*

Tetrachord	First appearance (bars)	Later appearances (bars)
B–C–E–F	opening to 68	349 358–402 421–91 924–25
D–E–G♯–A	105–56	157–200 (transposed) 442–91 (transposed) 523–24 (transposed) 559–79 (transposed) 689–92 (transposed) 923
E♭–A–B♭–D	543	554–55 (transposed) 702–6 (transposed) 889–92 (4 transposed versions)

'Indonesian' tetrachord (at b. 275), which in turn generates two long passages of frantic unison melody (Everett, forthcoming). Modest interconnections such as these give added shape to the more general, relaxed coherence lent by the work's predisposition towards four-note harmonies.

Delineating the Contents of *De Staat*

To judge from Andriessen's description of the compositional process for *De Staat*, formal proportions and tetrachordal harmonies were the principal factors controlling and marshalling his improvisatory explorations at the keyboard. But those explorations were themselves far from unstructured. Andriessen's 'playing and improvising' seems to have revolved around a limited number of types of material, and each of these gives particular expression to a facet of his wide-ranging interest in other musics. One should not imagine that these types of material necessarily formed conscious compositional concerns. Rather, they reflect recurrent preoccupations dogging his creative experimentation at the keyboard: a propensity for finding one's hands in a certain part of the keyboard, for instance, or playing around with a certain kind of material. Almost the entirety of the piece can be explained in terms of four loose categories, each of which recurs several times and helps to maintain the music's focus over its 35-minute span. These are:

(A) repetitive, mostly diatonic textures strongly redolent of American minimalism;
(B) frenetic unison melody;
(C) rhythmic, low-register, chromatic brass music;
(D) harshly dissonant chord sequences.

These recurrent 'basic ingredients' are underpinned by a more intricate network of references and repetitions that help keep the work's sudden transitions and startling contrasts in check. Table 3.2 lays out these interrelationships.

Of all the existing musics to which *De Staat* makes reference, American minimalism looms largest. *De Staat* is often thought of as a minimalist work. But some parts are more overtly indebted to American minimalism than others, and it is these that are labelled A in Table 3.2. In fact, no other work of Andriessen's pays such explicit homage, albeit intermittently, to all three of the major figures of American minimalism during the 1970s – Terry Riley, Steve Reich and Philip Glass.[9] This indebtedness is tentatively announced right from the start of the work, the subtly altered repetition of the first phrase and the close canons that follow recalling basic strategies of early American minimalism. Later (at b. 567), a more purist form of 'repetitive' music is evoked by a single five-note phrase, repeated no fewer than 74 times and slowly blurred as more instruments join in 'out of phase'. It is the lengthy tutti sections at bars 105–264 and 368–492, however, that provide the most idiomatic references to the sounds and spirit of works by Andriessen's American contemporaries. Here, as in most American minimalism from the mid-seventies, the music remains mostly diatonic,[10] adheres to a regular metre, and inhabits a (temporarily) reduced dynamic level. The energetic interlocking figuration of Reich's keyboard writing, the luxurious textures of Glass's *Music in Twelve Parts* and the relaxed hedonism of *In C* can all be perceived in these sections, combined in a distinctive cocktail that is one of *De Staat*'s most characteristic fingerprints.

---

[9] In a letter to the author (13 February 2003), Andriessen objected to part of this claim: 'I do not agree that Phil [Glass]'s early work has in any way influenced *De Staat*.' Andriessen had encountered Glass's music, however (see Ch. 2), so there remains the possibility of unconscious or unacknowledged influence; the musical evidence is quite strong for this.

[10] See Ch. 2 n. 8.

Table 3.2 *De Staat*: **formal summary**

Category	Bar	Timing	Description
(A)	1	0'00	white-note tetrachord (B–C–E–F)
C	68	2'09	chromatic trombones (+ horns at b. 87)
A	105	3'07	CHOIR I – 'dom. 7th' tetrachord (D–E–G♯–A)
A	157	4'51	'dom. 7th' tetrachord (G–A–C♯–D)
A	264	8'21	hectic ascending syncopations
B	275	8'43	fast unison melody – 'pelog bem' mode (A–B♭–D–E–F)
C	322	10'14	alternating bass chords
	337	10'34	… extended in triplets
D	349	10'53	dissonant chords (begins with white-note tetrachord); settles on treble cluster chord
A	358	11'16	white-note tetrachord (B–C–E–F); texture reminiscent of b. 170
(D)	403	12'41	interruption (brass)
A	409	12'53	eventually includes white-note and 'dom. 7th' tetrachords (F–B–C–E and F–G–B–C)
D	492	15'33	interruption; treble cluster chords
B	499	15'47	fast unison melody; settles onto 'pelog bem' mode (B–C–E–F♯–G)
C	516	16'20	alternating bass chords
(D)	518	16'29	ascending triplet chords
B	523	16'38	fast unison melody (modulating)
D	543	17'14	dissonant chords, accumulating (begins with E♭–A–B♭–D tetrachord)
(D)	552	17'32	triumphant bass-rooted chords
A	559	17'46	repeated five-note figure (contains 'dom. 7th' tetrachord – C–D–F♯–G)
(A)	580	19'19	CHOIR II
D	668	21'39	… treble cluster chords (cf. bb. 354–57)
(C)	694	22'46	… bass chords (cf. b. 516)
D	702	22'59	… accumulating chords (begins with G♭–C–D♭–F tetrachord)
	725	23'40	dissonant sextuplet crotchets ('Portato pesantissimo')
C	791	26'55	alternating bass chords (hocketing ensembles)

D	823	28'08	dissonant chords (cf. b. 322 and b. 516; last chord cf. b. 558)
(A)	840	28'43	'blues lick'
	867	29'15	ascending triplet chords (cf. b. 518)
A	873	29'27	hectic ascending syncopations (notes from b. 264, rhythm from b. 322)
D	889	29'50	dissonant tetrachords (see Ex. 3.5)
(A)	893	30'00	evolving diatonic scale (hocketing ensembles)
D	923	31'05	CHOIR III – starts with white-note tetrachord (B–F–C–E); moves to treble cluster chords
	951	32'44	canon, moving to unison

A number of more specific references may be identified in these two long sections. The sonority that launches the first – a dominant seventh on E with an added fourth (A) at the top of the chord – is a condensed version of the single harmony of Reich's *Four Organs* (see Ex. 3.2).[11] Given Andriessen's fondness for 'good bass notes' (see Koning and Jansen 1981, p. 14), it is not surprising that he should alight on the sole early minimalist work to root its processes with a strong bass. The music that follows, however – a sustained melodic line in voices and violas above buoyant repetitive figuration – has a more complex lineage. The immediate reference here is to Andriessen's own *Symphonies of the Netherlands* (1974) – a work that almost entirely lacks the grating tensions and drama of *De Staat*. The choir's stately melodic line, continued by the oboes at bar 170, is lifted practically verbatim from a passage about halfway through the *Symphonies*. A further stimulus was provided by a record of Javanese gamelan music from the court at Yogyakarta which Andriessen listened to 'a great deal' during the composition of *De Staat*

Ex. 3.2 Basic harmony of *Four Organs* and harmony at b. 105 of *De Staat*

Four Organs   De Staat

---

[11] I am indebted to Sam Hayden for pointing out this resemblance.

(Op de Coul 1979). It contained 'an amazing little women's choir singing long notes',[12] a sound that presumably encouraged the transplantation of the *Symphonies'* melodic line into a vocal context.

The counterpointing of repetitive figuration and sustained lines, crucial to both of these long sections of *De Staat*, may also be traced back to American minimalism. Riley's *In C* had established a precedent in this regard: the four semibreves at bar 14 of *In C* (the descending melodic line C–B–G–F♯) contrast starkly with the nervous figuration of surrounding bars, and are easily heard echoed in the first choral entry of *De Staat* and the similar texture from bar 368 (the melody line now in violas and horns).[13] Following the brass interruption at bar 403, however, the single melody line is discarded in favour of a less regimented assembly of soloistic melody and individually placed brass pedal notes. The immediate model here appears to be the swelling, gently dissonant sustained notes of Part Four of Glass's *Music in Twelve Parts* (1974). (Glass performed *Music in Twelve Parts* during his tour of Holland in 1975.[14]) In this passage the undulating scalic figuration in winds, guitars, pianos and harps also evokes Glass – and maybe also *In C*[15] – whereas the choppier repetitive patterns accompanying the oboe melody from bar 165 are more reminiscent of Reich's keyboard and percussion writing.

The impact of minimalism upon *De Staat* certainly does not end with these passages. But as we saw in Chapter 2, Andriessen's music during the seventies took a far from blithely uncritical stance towards American minimalism, and there is much in this work, too, that seeks to challenge its premises. *De Staat* offers, as it were, a set of positions in relation to minimalism, ranging from faithful homage to antagonistic refutation – a complex stance that receives more attention in Chapter 4. The second of the four categories of material outlined above, namely the extended passages of frenetic tutti unison melody that appear three times in the first half of the piece (labelled B in Table 3.2), represents a step along this continuum. The chromatic quality of these melodies, their unpredictable, improvisatory construction and their highly physical nature (which recalls the strenuous collective endeavour of *Workers Union*) marks them out as distinct from the majority of early minimalist compositions. On the other hand, there is a connection with the music of Frederic Rzewski,

---

[12] Letter to the author (4 April 2003).

[13] Compare the original 1968 recording of *In C* (issued on compact disc as CBS MK 7178) at 10'15.

[14] See the review of these concerts by Hans Heg: 'Glass zet geluidsmuur neer', *De Volkskrant*, 16 June 1975.

[15] Compare the original recording of *In C* at 24'00.

which, as we saw in Chapter 2, adapted minimalist techniques to distinctive ends. The technique deployed in Rzewski's *Les Moutons de Panurge*, of constructing a long unison melody by progressively adding more notes to a short repeated melodic phrase, was used again as the basis for his later piece *Coming Together* (1972), this time in a less strictly systematic fashion but with equal drive and vigour. It is *Coming Together* that forms the most immediate point of reference for *De Staat*.[16] In *Coming Together*, the melodic line is now decisively positioned in the bass register (Rzewski expressly requests a bass guitar).[17] This earthy quality – far removed from what Andriessen refers to as the 'cosmic nonsense' of much minimalism – is emphasized by an explicitly political meaning: the melody accompanies a recitation of phrases from a letter by a political prisoner.[18] The most obvious resonance of Rzewski's piece in *De Staat* is at the passage from bars 523 to 533 (see the extract from this passage in Ex. 3.3), but the additive patterns and nervous metrical games characterizing the entirety of Andriessen's long melodic lines testify to a more general influence.

Ex. 3.3   Unison melody (extract) of (a) *De Staat*, bb. 530–33, compared with (b) Rzewski, *Coming Together*, bb. 50–53

(a)

(b)

---

[16] Andriessen pointed this out in a letter to the author (13 February 2003). *Coming Together* featured prominently in the repertoire of Hoketus.

[17] See Rzewski's performing notes, reproduced in Cardew 1974, pp. 119–20.

[18] The author of the letter, Sam Melville, was killed during the 1971 riots at Attica Prison in New York State.

Another model also looms behind these sections of the work, one that reinforces the retreat from a strictly minimalist technique. Two-thirds of the way through the first movement of Berio's *Sinfonia* (1969), the braying, static orchestral harmonies and dense mesh of sung and spoken text that have dominated hitherto are relieved by the cautious emergence of a fragmentary melodic line on keyboards and harp. It gradually gains in confidence, building to a 'manic orchestral unison' (Osmond-Smith 1991, p. 18). As we saw in

Ex. 3.4   Unison melody (extract) of (a) Berio, *Sinfonia,* **1st mvt., bar before [J],**
compared with (b) *De Staat,* **bb. 282–302**

(a)

Chapter 1, Andriessen has a particular connection with *Sinfonia*, in that he introduced Berio to the recordings of the Swingle Singers, for whom *Sinfonia* was eventually written. In the unison melodies of *De Staat*, he may be seen as repaying the compliment (or collecting his due, depending on your perspective).[19] The hesitant silences of Berio's melody are absent in Andriessen's, but in a number of other ways Berio lays out precisely the parameters that Andriessen would follow (see Ex. 3.4(a)): the repetitive exploration of limited groups of pitches; the moments of insistent reiteration of a single interval or pitch; the dramatic pauses on a particular note; the angular intervals, and, particularly, the pervasive and characteristic minor ninth – an 'idée fixe' throughout this section (ibid., p. 19).[20] The two longer passages of unison

---

[19] In an interview given while writing *De Staat*, Andriessen comments on the use of unison in Berio's *Sinfonia*, without acknowledging a specific influence on his own work (Koopmans 1976b, p. 36).

[20] The role of the minor ninth in Andriessen's melodic writing will receive further attention below.

melody in *De Staat* (at bb. 275 and 499), in particular, share all of these characteristics (Ex. 3.4(b)).

The chromatic 'edge' of these melodic lines constitutes one of the ways in which *De Staat* offers a critique of the blander diatonicism of American minimalism. Fiercer comment still is passed by the last two general types of material outlined in Table 3.2. First, there is the aggressive, chromatic lower-register music whose abrupt first appearance at bar 68 following the tetrachordal opening section announces the most fundamental opposition (high, diatonic: low, chromatic) of all *De Staat*'s brusque juxtapositions. This type of material (labelled C in Table 3.2) mostly presents itself in the form of two fiercely alternating chords: an inhuman machine that stamps out whatever aspirations towards diatonic clarity the foregoing music may have had. (In so doing it re-enacts a similar gesture in *De Volharding*.[21]) The registral place-ment, harmonic content (typically derived from two superimposed diminished triads) and dramatic impact of these sections are strongly akin to the eleven brutal strokes that usher in the 'Glorification de l'élue' in *The Rite of Spring*. In places, this material is developed further: for instance in the asymmetrically accented triplets at bar 337, where the frenetic pace and muddy cluster chords emphasize parallels with *Workers Union*; and at bar 823, where a genetic fusion of the chords from bars 322 and 516 provides the starting point for a more grandiose, rhetorical statement.[22]

This last section in fact arguably belongs to the last of the four categories (labelled D in Table 3.2), a wide-ranging one accommodating the work's numerous passages of curdlingly dissonant chord sequences. These move the music forward in a variety of ways – effortful stepwise ascent (b. 349), a sort of accumulative 'clotting' (b. 543; b. 702), or sheer free-wheeling registral abandon (b. 889). In several cases Andriessen animates these chord sequences with rasping flutter-tongues or insistent repeated-note figuration – the latter perhaps derived from the reiterative brass toccatas in the 'Euntes mundum' and 'Illi autem profecti' of Stravinsky's *Canticum Sacrum* (which in turn pays homage to the antiphonal brass music of the early Venetian Baroque).

The loose coherence that these four categories give to the work is enhanced by Andriessen's strategies of transition. Despite his adherence to the Stravinskian formal principle of abrupt juxtaposition – in Chapter 5 Andriessen talks of his desire that the piece should be 'shocking and surprising and sudden' – new sections are by no means always unprepared or without

---

[21] 14'47 on the recording of *De Volharding*.

[22] The sketches show that Andriessen originally intended a recapitulation of the alternating chords at this point.

linear logic. They are typically heralded, for instance, by a dramatic crescendo; the long hairpins gracing the top of numerous pages of the score – sometimes additionally marked 'molto', or even 'massimo crescendo' – are a reliable indicator of the sectional structure of the music. The music's constant crotchet speed (crotchet = 126–132 throughout, except at bb. 840–66 where there is a temporary 'più mosso') provides consistency between sections. Additionally, successive sections are often tethered by an element of registral continuity. This is the case, for instance, at bar 403 where the happy diatonic burblings of one of *De Staat*'s longer minimalist passages are terminated by an aggressive brass entry – whose uppermost note (a high A) has nevertheless been well prepared by the high G in the preceding section (see Ex. 3.1). Pitch adjacencies of this sort may bind a number of contrasting sections of music. Between bars 322 and 358 the uppermost notes of four distinct sections spell out a gradual stepwise ascent, from F above middle C to the F an octave higher; this line binds (in a typically Stravinskian gesture) the chain of chromatic chords of bar 349 as well as the various sections that surround it. A similar gradual ascent binds the passage between bars 840 and 889.[23]

A network of more specific repetitions and allusions underpins the elements of general continuity and contrast discussed so far. As Table 3.1 and Ex. 3.1 make clear, the music leading up to both the second and third choral sections is particularly rich in interconnection. The first of these passages commences just after bar 492, with two clustered tetrachords that recall the similarly clotted harmonies in the final bars before bar 358 – borrowing, more specifically, both registral placement and general pitch content (white-note harmony with a lower E♭ and upper C♯ – see Ex. 3.1). This is one of the most distinctive recurrent sonorities of the work. It appears again in the middle of the second choral passage at bar 668, this time with a low F pedal note; and it dominates the latter stages of the choir's final statement (b. 945). Indeed, the whole of the final choral section can be seen as struggling its way towards a rearticulation of this pervasive, closely registered harmony.

The initial recurrence of this harmony at bar 492 triggers a separate sequence of recapitulatory and anticipatory gestures. First, the unison melody at bar 499, following a chromatic, 'furioso' opening, gradually settles into a condensed recapitulation (transposed) of the unison melody at bar 275

---

[23] A couple of passages near the end of Stravinsky's *Symphony of Psalms* (see [25] and [28]) provide the model for this ubiquitous gesture (in Andriessen's music) of a slowly rising melodic line supported by a chain of chromatic chords. The end of *Contra Tempus* provides an early example in a thoroughly atonal context; the closing stages of *De Stijl* include a more recognizably Stravinskian version (see b. 591 ff.).

(compare the harmonies at bb. 277 and 503). This in turn plunges into a slightly altered repetition of the aggressively alternating bass-register chords from bar 322. The staccato triplets that follow soon after (b. 519) are themselves recapitulated at bar 867, during the busy run-up to the work's final choral section. Similarly, the accumulating chords at bar 543 find an echo in the final part of the second choral section (b. 702).

Just as this nexus of references is used to prepare the re-entry of the choir at bar 580, so the choir's final statement is preceded by a rush of allusion and repetition. As I mentioned earlier, a combination of the chords from bars 322 and 516 triggers the rather Kentonesque tutti at bar 823. The last chord of this statement, however (b. 839), is clearly related to the chord (at b. 558) that ushers in the endlessly repeated pentachord prior to the second choral section. The accelerating 'blues lick' (as Andriessen calls it)[24] that follows (at b. 840) is then abruptly cut off by the altered reprise of the triplets from bar 519. This leads to a repeat of the straining ascent of bar 264 – in fact, the most literal recapitulation in the whole work, even though strictly speaking the rhythm here derives from the pounding lower-register music at bar 322 rather than bar 264 itself. Appropriately, the first of the chain of tetrachords at bar 889 is a transposition of the chord at bar 275.

In terms of actual pitches, however, this first chord at bar 889 refers more immediately to the triumphant instrumental climax (b. 552) preceding the second choral section. The second chord at bar 889 strengthens this latter allusion, for it is identical with the subsequent chord in the earlier passage (b. 554). In fact, as Ex. 3.5 shows, each of the first seven of the tetrachords at bars 889–92 alludes to a different part of the work – a sort of rapid summary of the piece, before it proceeds to its decisive closing stages. So, the third chord briefly points to the superimposed tritones of bar 791 (albeit in transposition); the fourth reminds us of the white-note tetrachord that began the work and reappeared regularly thereafter; and the fifth, sixth and seventh

Ex. 3.5   *De Staat*: tetrachords at bb. 889–92

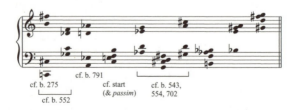

---

[24] Letter to the author (13 February 2003).

all present the tetrachordal configuration (in various transpositions) that begins the accumulating chords at bars 543 and 702.

In the context of this maze of references, the broad hocketing melody (at b. 893 ff.) that acts as a bridge to the final choral section seems especially majestic and unprecedented, signalling, as it were, that the work's main business is being brought to a close. The very final section, too – in which the two halves of the ensemble engage in a furious canon[25] – is quite unprecedented, a provocative rebuttal of the tendencies to interconnection apparent elsewhere. It thus symbolizes Andriessen's ambivalence about self-contained formal design, a self-containedness towards which *De Staat* sometimes leans but which it never fully endorses.

Modes

In his programme note to the recording of *De Staat*, Andriessen declares that the piece 'has nothing to do with Greek music, except perhaps for the use of oboes and harps and for the fact that the entire work is based on tetrachords' (Andriessen 1977b, p. 43). The reason he might feel it necessary to make such a statement is, of course, that the Plato text is itself a commentary on the music of the time, and a detailed one at that: different modes and instruments are examined for their moral character and their suitability for the ideal state. As such, it invites a musical setting that 'illustrates' the specifics of Socrates' dialogue with his pupil Glaucon. In fact, Andriessen's music establishes no such obvious relation with the text. (That is not to say that the music has *no* stake in the broader themes with which Plato was concerned, as I will discuss further in the next chapter.) *De Staat* engages with too wide a range of preoccupations for it to confine itself to evocations of ancient musical practices or representations of Plato's characterization of those practices. On the specific question of modes, Andriessen has said, 'I would be very reluctant to use the word modes for *De Staat*. In my opinion harmonies (or melodies) of more than four notes are tetrachords with added notes from another tetrachord.'[26]

Why, then, pursue the issue of modes in relation to *De Staat*? One reason is that the work's composition certainly did not proceed in complete ignorance of Greek modal theory. Two pages of the sketches to *De Staat* contain a transcription of parts of a short essay on ancient Greek modes and musical

---

[25] This section of the work receives fuller discussion in Ch. 4.

[26] Letter to the author (13 February 2003).

instruments by Arnold van Akkeren. (Van Akkeren's essay was later included in the notes to the first LP recording of *De Staat*.[27]) In copying out the modes described by Van Akkeren, Andriessen added his own modest analytical annotations highlighting their intervallic structure; this suggests that he had more than a passing interest in the harmonic practice of ancient Greek musicians. In Chapter 5, Andriessen explains these sketch pages as part of the process of reading and reflection that precedes any large composition: they should not be presumed to correspond to anything in the finished work. But at the very least the sketches show that an understanding of Greek music theory formed a backdrop to the work's genesis.

A further reason for approaching *De Staat* in terms of modes is that it is directly influenced by another modal musical tradition: that of the Javanese gamelan. In addition to the textural references described earlier, *De Staat* also contains several references to the distinctive 'pelog' mode of the Javanese gamelan, as I discuss further below. More generally, Andriessen's distinctive approach to diatonic materials frequently involves (for instance) the flattened sevenths and raised fourths common in jazz and American minimalism, and thus often responds well to modal analysis. Modes of course feature prominently in analytical discussions of both jazz and minimalism.[28]

A number of commentators have made modest attempts to identify 'modal' elements in *De Staat*. Maja Trochimczyk, for instance, points to the conjunction, at the start of the piece, of a 'Phrygian fragment B–C–E–F' and a 'Lydian … tetrachord of D–E–G♯–A'. She proposes a link to the Plato text by describing these modal fragments as 'permitted' and 'forbidden' respectively, in line with Plato's descriptions of these modes (Trochimczyk (ed.) 2002, p. 103). Timothy Johnson concurs with Trochimczyk, identifying the D–E–G♯–A tetrachord dominating the opening choral section as Lydian (Johnson 1994, p. 758). Gisela Gronemeyer comments in more general terms on Andriessen's use of the Mixolydian mode, intended (she suggests) as a refutation of Plato's description of this mode as 'weakening to the character' (Gronemeyer 1992, p. 56). None of these writers, however, draws attention to

---

[27] This note is reproduced in Van Akkeren 1977. Van Akkeren, a specialist in Greek music, was, in Andriessen's words, his 'guru' on the subject. In addition to the issues already mentioned, Van Akkeren advised Andriessen on the rhythmic enunciation of the Plato extracts set in *De Staat*'s central choral section (see Ch. 5).

[28] For instance, Mark C. Gridley lists all the church modes and many non-Western modes in the Appendix to his basic jazz primer (Gridley 2000, pp. 435–37), and Keith Potter's analyses of early American minimalism make frequent recourse to modal categories (Potter 2000, *passim*).

an important consideration when assessing the music's modal structure in the light of Plato's discussion: namely, the fact that the ancient Greek modes do not correspond to the system of 'Church' modes with which we are familiar today. Van Akkeren's account, transcribed in the sketches to *De Staat*, demonstrates this very clearly. What Van Akkeren refers to as the Dorian mode (represented by the scale from E to E on the white notes of the keyboard) corresponds to the Phrygian Church mode; his Phrygian (the white-note scale from D to D) corresponds to the Dorian; and so on.[29] The medieval theorists who developed the system of Church modes as a way of organizing the huge repertory of liturgical chant in use during the tenth and eleventh centuries borrowed many of the Greek modal names, but attributed them to the 'wrong' scales.[30] Additionally, it is now believed that the modes of Plato's time were also significantly different from the diatonic modes described by Van Akkeren, which represent the modal theory of *late* antiquity. The modes familiar to Plato, many centuries earlier, had little connection with each other (in contrast to the cyclically related diatonic modes), and they also included microtonal intervals (Barker 1984, p. 165 ff.; West 1992, pp. 164–65). In this light, Andriessen's intuition, expressed in Chapter 5, that the Greek scales described by Van Akkeren were not sufficiently 'exotic' for his purposes is, unwittingly, an accurate reflection of the facts of the matter.

Thus, any analysis of *De Staat* that takes the Church modes as its primary terms of reference is immediately far removed from the modal categories and associations discussed by Plato. This does not render such analyses useless; my own assessment of modal structure will stick to the modern categories. But it is important to be clear that no connection with the Plato text is being assumed. There is a second respect in which the analytical observations of Trochimczyk and Johnson need to be treated with caution, and that has to do with the way in which they set about establishing the modal identity of groups of pitches. In theory, any group of pitches from the diatonic scale could belong to any of the diatonic modes. What allows us to distinguish between them is the way in which those pitches are deployed in a given musical context, and,

---

[29] In total, Van Akkeren equates Dorian to the (white-note) E scale, Phrygian to the D scale, Mixolydian to the B scale, Lydian to the C scale and Ionian to the G scale; see 'Ancient Greek music'. Andriessen alludes to the difference between 'Christian' and 'Greek' modes in his lecture on *Rosa* (in Andriessen 1998b, p. 250), although the details are a bit confused.

[30] A recent, comprehensive explanation of how this happened is given in David E. Cohen, 'Notes, scales, and modes in the earlier Middle Ages', in Thomas Christensen (ed.), *The Cambridge History of Western Music Theory* (Cambridge: Cambridge University Press, 2002), pp. 307–63; see pp. 331–38.

specifically, the way in which one of the pitches takes the role of 'final' – roughly equivalent to the tonic in tonal music. So, Trochimczyk's reading of the opening section as Phrygian assumes that the E is the governing 'final', the four pitches (B–C–E–F) spelling out the fifth, sixth, first and second pitches respectively of the Phrygian Church mode on E. There is, however, little to support this interpretation of E as the final: it receives no special emphasis at any point in the opening section. Viewed in isolation, the ascending tetrachord B–C–E–F would be better treated as a Locrian collection, with the lowest note of the four pitches (that is, B) taking on the role of 'final' – the role performed by the lowest note in the authentic modes of liturgical chant. This is the form in which these four notes reappear at bar 358 in *De Staat*. But at the opening of the work, it is F that seems pivotal: F is the lowest note of the opening chord; and it is the 'destination' pitch of many of the section's ascending phrases. The remaining pitches – the dominant (C), leading note (E) and the distinctive raised fourth (B) – spell out the *Lydian* mode on F.

Modal analysis depends, therefore, on the identification of the 'final' of any given passage. In Andriessen's music there is often more ambiguity about the identity of the 'final' than in (for instance) liturgical plainchant or pop music. The first choral section is a case in point. Trochimczyk's and Johnson's reading of this section as Lydian treats the D as the 'final'. However, the powerful bass octave E that marks the start of the section arguably resonates as a fundamental pitch throughout the whole passage. (Andriessen's sketches reveal, startlingly, that at one stage he contemplated periodic reiterations of the bass E while the choir is singing.) If E is taken as the final, then the tetrachord D–E–G♯–A articulates the flattened seventh, major third and perfect fourth of the Mixolydian mode. Alternatively, one could follow David Wright and treat A as the vocal line's 'nodal pitch' (Wright 1993, p. 9): many of the choir's melodic phrases begin and end on repeated or sustained As, and the section as a whole ends on a long, held A. In this case, the tetrachord would spell out the perfect fourth, fifth, leading note and tonic of the Ionian mode – our modern-day 'major scale'. (In the following discussion I have opted for a Mixolydian interpretation of this passage.)

With such considerations in mind, as well as an eye to the fact that much of *De Staat* is agressively chromatic and resists modal interpretation altogether, it is nevertheless possible to construct an overview of Andriessen's use of modes in *De Staat* (see the boxed labels on Ex. 3.1). Before commenting on the longer-term harmonic trends that this reveals, some points of detail deserve mention. For instance, the work's most significant tetrachords, discussed earlier in this chapter, sometimes undergo modal transformations. The reappearance of the four notes of the opening (Lydian) section as a Locrian tetrachord at bar 358 has already been noted. The Lydian potential of these pitches re-emerges, however, from bar 442, where a bass F is increasingly confidently asserted. The Mixolydian tetrachord of the first choral section is similarly recast at later stages: in fact, as early as bar 170 it takes on a Lydian quality (the 'seventh' of the set now rooting the accompanimental harmony, and repeatedly returned to by the melodic line). A further Lydian version of this harmony, now transposed, emerges at bar 523. Finally, the repeated pentachord (C–D–G–F♯–A) at bar 567 – which contains the same tetrachord – also takes a Lydian form, although the powerful octave As in the bass that mark its introduction eight bars previously initially suggest the Dorian mode (A–C–E–F♯–G).

The sense of urgent anxiety conveyed by the work's passages of frantic unison melody may partly be accounted for on modal grounds. It is in these passages that the harmonic influence of the Javanese gamelan is most clearly evident. Javanese gamelan orchestras use two basic types of tuning: one, 'slendro', is pentatonic and corresponds roughly to the interval structure of the black notes on the piano keyboard; the other, 'pelog', comprises a seven-note scale roughly equivalent to the interval structure of the Phrygian mode (Powers and Perlman 2001, pp. 844–46).[31] In practice, only five of the seven notes of pelog are used for any one piece. In the case of gamelan music from Yogyakarta (the tradition Andriessen was interested in at the time of writing *De Staat*), the 'pelog bem' mode omits note 7 altogether, and treats note 4 as a possible substitute for notes 3 or 5. The version of the pelog bem mode without this substitution – C, D♭, E♭, G, A♭ – has appeared in several Western evocations of the gamelan, including Poulenc's Concerto for Two Pianos (1932) and Britten's *The Prince of the Pagodas* (1959) (Cooke 1998).[32] Andriessen, however, takes the option of substituting the fourth note for the third, resulting in a scale comprising the first, second, fourth, fifth and sixth degrees of the Phrygian mode. This scale is first used at bar 275 (A–B♭–D–E–F), and although it is soon joined by further pitches that cannot be explained in terms of the Javanese model, these five notes remain to the fore throughout this lengthy passage (bb. 275–321). Similarly, the second

---

[31] Comparisons are very approximate as all gamelans are slightly differently tuned, and none corresponds precisely to the degrees of the chromatic scale. Powers and Perlman focus on Surakartan traditions; however, the 'pelog nem' and 'pelog lima' tunings that they describe correspond in practice to the pelog bem of Yogyakarta.

[32] In both these cases, the composers were in fact adopting the Balinese equivalent of the pelog bem mode; the basic pitches are similar, but the registral arrangement is different.

passage of unison semiquaver melody (b. 499), while commencing with non-diatonic patterns, quickly settles into a loose (and shortened) recapitulation of the earlier 'pelog bem' melody, transposed up a tone. Other passages of the piece can also be derived from Javanese modes: for instance, the opening choral phrase corresponds to the first four notes of the 'pelog barang' mode (notes 2, 3, 5, 6 and 7 of the Phrygian scale). Andriessen's use of pelog bem remains more distinctive, however, partly perhaps because its greater distance from conventional tonal harmonies, combined with the inauthentically unyielding vigour of its treatment, sound like an act of deliberate resistance to American minimalism's more anodyne reception of Indonesian music.[33]

Some more general harmonic trends may be discerned from the appearances of the diatonic modes in *De Staat*. In the first half of the work, the Lydian mode is particularly prominent. It is heard at the very beginning of the piece, and thereafter returns regularly and for significant periods. It dominates both the second half of the long, overtly 'minimalist' passage at bars 409–91, and (in various different forms and on different pitches) the giddy lead-up to the second choral section (bb. 523–79). The importance of the Lydian mode in *De Staat* resonates with the established role it, and more particularly its characteristic sharpened fourth, has in jazz. Sharpened fourths are common in jazz, partly as a result of the familiar augmented eleventh extension to a dominant seventh. In modal terms, this chord belongs to the 'acoustic' scale (flattened seventh as well as sharpened fourth) rather than one of the diatonic modes, but the affinity of this scale to the Lydian mode is underlined by its alternative designation 'Lydian dominant' in jazz terminology. On a larger scale, the proposal by the writer and musician George Russell that pitch relations in jazz improvisation should be based on the Lydian mode rather than the major scale had a considerable influence on the development of modal jazz from the end of the fifties onwards (Brubeck 2002, pp. 190–92).[34] The Lydian mode is also prominent in some minimal music. In the middle of Riley's *In C*, for instance, F♯s temporarily replace F♮s, yet C remains identifiably the tonic; at this moment the piece is not so much 'in C', as 'in C-Lydian' (Potter 2000, pp. 113–14).

From the second choral section of *De Staat* onwards, however, the influence of the Lydian mode wanes: the only further significant use of the

---

[33] Steve Reich took lessons on the Balinese gamelan from native musicians in the summers of 1973 and 1974 (Potter 2000, p. 207). It should not be forgotten that Indonesia was a Dutch colony until 1949.

[34] Russell's book was entitled *The Lydian Chromatic Concept of Tonal Organization* (1953).

mode occurs in the final section of the work (b. 951), and here extra pitches quickly move the music out of the diatonic realm. The principal appearances of the Phrygian and related 'pelog bem' modes are also confined to the work's first half. Indeed, in general there is less diatonic music in the work's later stages. If there is one mode that gains in importance in the second half of the piece, it is the Aeolian mode – the natural minor scale. After making a temporary appearance in two of the long, 'minimalist' sections in the work's first half (at bb. 201 and 415 respectively) the Aeolian mode does not reappear until the second choral section, where it gives a grave seriousness to Plato's strictures on musical practice. Even here we only hear the first four notes of the scale, plus a rogue A♮; but Andriessen's reintroduction of this mode, with its strong minor-key resonances, at this critical point in the work signals a shift in harmonic emphasis away from the optimistic Lydian that has dominated up to this point. The new importance of the Aeolian mode is underlined when it is gradually unfolded in the hocketing melody at bar 893, immediately before the final choral statement. This is the first and only sustained melodic exploration of the complete diatonic collection in the entire work, a temporary clearing of all modal ambiguity and chromatic complication, at least until a last-minute G♯ knocks things off kilter. Having withheld it for so long, the effect of introducing the full diatonic scale at this late stage is highly dramatic. In ways such as these, Andriessen's subtle handling of diatonic materials constitutes an important shaping force on the work as a whole.

Tonality

The particular importance of the Aeolian mode towards the end of *De Staat* serves as a reminder that tonality is a crucial element of much of Andriessen's music, and that no discussion of *De Staat* would be adequate without considering the extent to which tonal organization plays a part. In keeping faith, as *De Staat* does, with the spirit of social critique that drove the Orkest De Volharding, it was inevitable that the music should, as Andriessen says in Chapter 5, 'avoid a lot of the tonal things … the whole idea [was] to be provocative and aggressive and not nice and sweet'. However, to write music that completely avoided contact with tonality had, since the late sixties, been equally unthinkable. Andriessen strove for a music that, like Stravinsky, was 'tonal, but at the same time non-tonal' (Andriessen and Schönberger 1989, p. 100). Triads and conventional chord progressions are completely avoided. But, as we saw in the previous section, there are many passages in *De Staat* dominated by diatonic harmonies, which inevitably lend a tonal 'sound' to the

music. Andriessen's 'good bass notes', wielded sparingly though they are –
each one acting as a mighty anchor for the music around it – provide a remnant
of the sort of functional differentiation between bass and treble registers
characteristic of tonality. And, despite the music's countless abrupt disruptions
and juxtapositions, voice-leading (crucial in ensuring the linear continuity
characteristic of tonality) is not entirely ignored – as we have already seen
with the smoothly ascending upper lines linking successive sections at various
stages. Various elements of *De Staat*, then, encourage a tonal interpretation.

Crucial, though, to the work's 'tonal and yet non-tonal' quality is the role
played by harmonies made up of notes derived from a diatonic scale with the
addition of a single chromatic note. Harmonies of this sort are common in
Andriessen's works: some prominent examples from other works of the
seventies and early eighties are shown in Ex. 3.6.[35] The principle can be related
to the 'blue notes' that supplement the diatonic scale in blues and jazz; as we
saw in Chapter 2, these were already a significant feature of Andriessen's early
works for De Volharding. In *De Staat*, three of the four possible eight-note
harmonies that include the diatonic scale[36] are articulated at important
moments towards the end of the work, as if to signify their importance to the
sound of the piece overall. The eight notes heard between bars 873 and 888,
and again (transposed) between bars 893 and 922, stand out particularly, for
they comprise the 'diatonic octad' – so called because it includes *two* different
diatonic scales (Straus 1990, p. 96). The diatonic octad thus tends towards
bitonality, a property extensively exploited in music by Stravinsky and other

**Ex. 3.6   Harmonies derived from diatonic scale with addition of one chromatic
note: some examples in Andriessen's music**

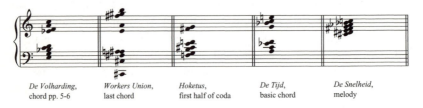

| *De Volharding,* | *Workers Union,* | *Hoketus,* | *De Tijd,* | *De Snelheid,* |
| chord pp. 5-6 | last chord | first half of coda | basic chord | melody |

---

[35] See also Andriessen and Harsh 1992, p. 64.

[36] It might seem that the twelve-note chromatic scale should provide *five* different
options (not four) for adding a note to the seven-note diatonic scale. But two of these
options (adding a sharpened fourth or a flattened seventh to the major scale) in fact
result in the same basic harmony – an eight-note slice from the cycle of fifths – albeit
in different transpositions. I am very grateful to Tom Hall for important suggestions
regarding this section of my discussion.

composers.[37] The other two eight-note sets at the end of *De Staat* are more redolent of the blues. The pitches between bars 867 and 872 spell out what Larry Solomon terms 'blues mode 2' – equivalent to the Dorian mode with added flattened fifth (Solomon 2003). The eight notes that predominate at the start of the final canon, meanwhile, comprise simply the major scale plus the 'blue' flattened third. Ex. 3.7 shows each of these distinctive eight-note harmonies, as well as a number of smaller harmonies from earlier in the work whose diatonic component is similarly 'complicated' by a single chromatic note. This chromatic inflection of a basic diatonic collection gives *De Staat* much of its distinctive harmonic flavour.

In passing, it is worth noting that Andriessen tends to adopt registral arrangements of these harmonies that highlight the chromatic dissonance. A particularly favoured arrangement involves placing the dissonant note in an outer registral position, to form a minor ninth with another part of the harmony

Ex. 3.7   *De Staat*: **harmonies derived from diatonic scale with addition of one chromatic note**

<hr>

[37] For instance, Allen Forte has observed that this harmony is 'the master diatonic set' in *The Rite of Spring* (*The Harmonic Organization of The Rite of Spring* (New Haven: Yale University Press, 1978), p. 140), and Paul Johnson has identified numerous instances throughout Stravinsky's oeuvre ('Cross-collectional techniques of structure in Stravinsky's centric music', in Ethan Haimo and Paul Johnson (eds), *Stravinsky Retrospectives* (Lincoln: University of Nebraska Press, 1987), pp. 55–75). Elliott Antokoletz, meanwhile, has pointed to the importance of the harmony in works by Bartók (*The Music of Béla Bartók* (Berkeley: University of California Press, 1982), p. 206 ff.).

(see Ex. 3.8). The tendency of *De Staat*'s hectic unison melodies to get jammed on an insistent, rocking minor ninth has already been noted in this chapter, and Andriessen's penchant for this interval is symbolized by the defiant upward minor ninth that brings the work to a close.

Ex. 3.8   *De Staat*: **prominent minor 9ths (indicated with bracket) in harmonies derived from diatonic scale with addition of one chromatic note (empty notehead)**

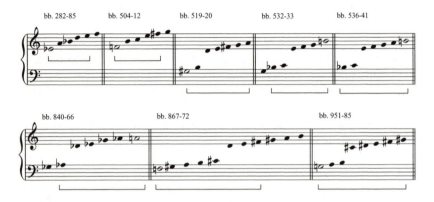

The prevalence of near-diatonic harmonies facilitates the emergence of two important, albeit intermittent tonal features: namely, centricity (that is, the attribution to a particular pitch of a privileged or governing role) and functionality (the attribution of particular roles to different harmonies on the basis of accustomed patterns of succession in the tonal repertoire). The term 'tonic' has particular connotations in relation to traditional tonality; I will use it here simply to indicate pitches strongly projected as roots of particular diatonic or near-diatonic pitch collections. At both the beginning and end of *De Staat*, such tonics emerge clearly and are sometimes prolonged across more than one section, helping to provide an element of stability that subtly grounds the work as a whole. As we have seen, the beginning of the piece asserts F as the 'tonic' of a Lydian tetrachord. But tonally speaking this is by way of a prologue: the Phrygian cadence that ends this first section, onto a chord rooted on E, anticipates the bolder and more conventionally tonal emphases on E at the first choral entry and (more ambiguously) at bar 264 (see Ex. 3.9(a)).[38] An imposing bass E also roots the final choral passage, and it

---

[38] Aspects of Exx. 3.9 and 3.10 vaguely resemble Schenkerian diagrams, but they are not intended to invoke Schenkerian concepts.

Ex. 3.9 Implied tonics (a) at start of *De Staat*; (b) at end of *De Staat*

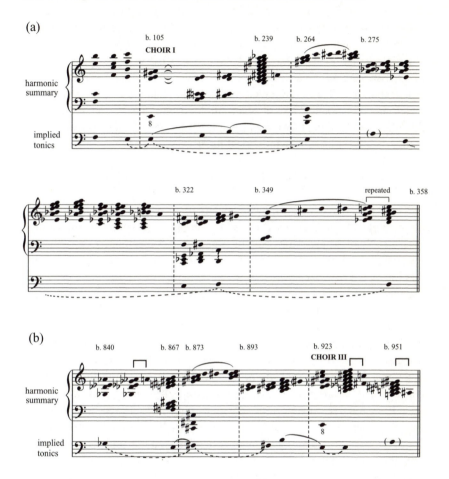

continues to resonate through the whole section by virtue of the Es prominent at the top of the chords that follow (Ex. 3.9(b)). These emphases on E form a basic tonal frame for the whole work. The closing canon then forms a sort of epilogue (initially suggesting A Lydian), mirroring the F Lydian prologue of the opening.

Further areas of tonic continuity appear adjacent to each assertion of E (see Ex. 3.9). As the 'pelog bem' melody at bar 275 proceeds, its A Phrygian quality recedes somewhat in favour of a D minor tonality (the lower E♭ acting as a chromatic neighbour note). D remains prominent in the noisy lower-register material that follows (bb. 322–48), before finally being asserted more

confidently as a tonic in the repeated chords at bar 357. D thus succeeds E as
the music's focal pitch. Similarly, the 'blues lick' that ushers in the closing
stages of *De Staat* (at b. 840) establishes a G flat melodic-minor tonality,[39]
which is reiterated (as F sharp minor) twice in subsequent sections. Following
a short passage elaborating an E7 chord (or VII7 in F sharp minor), the
upward-striving semiquavers at bar 873 return with a second-inversion F sharp
minor sonority. This is reinforced by the broad diatonic melody at bar 893,
which initially sounds like F sharp minor (until the B and G♮ effect a
modulation to B minor). Taken as a whole, then, the outermost sections of the
work articulate a broadly symmetrical tonal structure:

Lydian prologue – E – D … F♯ – E – Lydian epilogue

The central parts of the work contain less in the way of long-term emphases
on particular tonics; they revel instead in abrupt juxtaposition and unexpected
contrast of all kinds. However, the dizzying momentum created by one
passage in particular (from b. 516 to the entry of the choir at b. 580) is such
that one is led to wonder whether it can be explained by rhythmic drive and
incidental excitement alone. In Chapter 5 Andriessen says that he was not
much concerned with tonal functions at the time of *De Staat*; it seems that he
developed an interest in the potential of tonal syntax only relatively late in
life.[40] Yet this section of *De Staat* sounds tonal in a deeper sense than those
discussed so far – which is to say, it seems sensitive and responsive to the
functional implications of different chords. Characteristically, the more
conventional tonal progressions are avoided. An attempt to extract the
underlying tonal harmonies in this passage points instead to the importance of
root movement by thirds (see Ex. 3.10). The pounding, lower-register music at
bar 516 loosely articulates a C minor collection, and this tonic is carried over
into the second-inversion C harmony (with the raised, Lydian fourth so
characteristic of the piece) at bar 518. This chord marks the beginning of an
unusually rapid series of harmonic shifts. First, the C Lydian chord is replaced

---

[39] Andriessen interprets this section differently, arguing that, considered as a 'blues
lick', it is 'in E-flat minor, with the world-famous flattened fifth' (letter to the author,
13 February 2003). I find it harder to hear the passage in these terms, although such an
interpretation highlights the connection between this passage and the first half of the
second choral section (b. 580).

[40] In 2000, Andriessen said, 'A note is only right because of what went before it and
because of the following note; the harmony only has to do with the harmony before and
after it. That is what I am beginning to understand after a long life' (Andriessen 2000,
p. 316).

Ex. 3.10 *De Staat*: **underlying harmonies at bb. 503–80**

by staccato triplets outlining an E major-minor collection – thereby returning to the implied tonic of the melodic material preceding the alternating bass chords. Then this is succeeded in turn by a further major-minor harmony at bar 522, this time on G♯ (with added second in the root). The G♯ tonic is held over into the A♭ Lydian of the resuming semiquaver melody. As a whole, then, this passage spells out two consecutive major-third harmonic shifts – from C to E to G♯.

Similar progressions appear again shortly afterwards. The unison melody begun at bar 523 proceeds through a couple of dominant harmonies to culminate (at b. 541) on an F Lydian collection. The accumulating chords that follow retain a connection with F, the low C and high F eventually confirming an F7 harmony that links smoothly – by ascending major third – to the triumphant A major (with added sixth) at bar 552. Further movement by thirds, this time descending, connects the next two chords: here a G♭ Lydian harmony slips to a D major-minor seventh chord. This latter harmony acts as a preparation for the repeated pentachord at bar 559. However, the dominant function of this pentachord is enhanced by the chord that immediately precedes it – an augmented sixth chord, in essence, of the sort so often used to prepare dominants in nineteenth-century tonal harmony.[41] In the event, the dominant is never resolved, but shifts back instead to the flattened sixth degree to form a kind of interrupted cadence at the entry of the choir (b. 580).

Andriessen prefers to see these harmonic connections in terms of transpositions, rather than as instances of functional tonal syntax (see Ch. 5). On the other hand, the chords are clearly *not* literal transpositions of each other, their similarities notwithstanding. His adoption of this harmonic strategy might be traced instead to the post-Wagnerian French composers whose music he came to know so well as a child (see Ch. 1); like many other late nineteenth-century composers, Franck, Fauré and Chausson made much use of third-based harmonic relations.[42] Equally, one can hear pop music behind this harmonic trait. Where the Romantics tended to conceive of thirds relations in terms of transcendent spirituality, pop – in which tonic cadences from the flattened sixth degree, producing the same upward major-third progression, are common – reinterprets them as a marker of raunchy physicality.[43] Either way, the progression of harmonic areas in this passage sounds 'logical' by virtue of our familiarity with similar patterns in a range of other music. It is here that *De Staat* comes closest to traditional tonality. Andriessen's complex, non-triadic harmonies remind us, though, that the

---

[41] Alternatively, this 'augmented sixth' might be read as an altered version of the 'substitute dominant' of jazz harmony – a dominant-seventh formation built on the flattened second degree of the scale. This would mean treating the repeated dominant seventh that follows as a 'tonic' resolution, rather than the dominant function implied by the augmented sixth.

[42] Thirds relations in works by these three composers receive attention in, respectively, Richard Cohn, 'Maximally smooth cycles, hexatonic systems, and the analysis of late-Romantic triadic progressions', *Music Analysis*, **15** (1996), 26–27; Carlo Caballero, *Fauré and French Musical Aesthetics* (Cambridge: Cambridge University Press, 2001), pp. 236–37; Steven Huebner, *French Opera at the Fin de Siècle: Wagnerism, Nationalism and Style* (Oxford: Oxford University Press, 1999), pp. 390–92.

[43] The use of this cadence in pop music can be connected to the unavailability of the major dominant triad in certain modal contexts; see Björnberg 1984. In jazz, major-third relations have come to be known as 'Coltrane changes' or 'giant steps', following Coltrane's adventurous exploration of third-related harmonic regions in his 1959 track 'Giant Steps'. However, Coltrane prefers not to juxtapose directly chords a major third apart, preferring instead to precede each 'structural' chord with a secondary dominant; see Strunk 2002, p. 170.

certainties of tonal function are (to say the least) hard-won in this musical context, and carry no privileged role in relation to harmony elsewhere in the piece.

This moment of more ambitious tonal ordering can be seen as belonging to a broad community of types of coherence in *De Staat*. As I have attempted to show in this chapter, this community works at a variety of levels. Architectural stability is provided by the work's three choral 'caryatids', the framing tonics, and the gradual shift as the work proceeds from a preponderance of Lydian harmonies to Aeolian ones. At a more local level, Andriessen's Stravinskian collage of recognizable types of material manages to sustain a sense of urgent purpose without ever slipping into formulaic predictability. And his fondness for diatonic and near-diatonic harmonies lends a general consistency, one that is also accommodating of subtle differentiation – and (with the music's rawest chromatic dissonances) periodic harsher contrast. These various binding factors rub up against the elements of fortuity, spontaneity and risk by means of which Andriessen attempts to keep himself well removed from prevailing compositional orthodoxies.

   In the final section of Chapter 4 this tense relationship between formal propriety and rowdy impetuosity will be viewed in the context of Andriessen's interest in entering into a 'dialectical relationship' with other concert-hall music. *De Staat* attempts to keep order and anarchy in precipitous balance. But this is only one of several ways in which the piece requires to be viewed in terms of its broader context. As I noted at the start of this chapter, there is much in *De Staat* that encourages us to direct our attention beyond the music's internal workings and towards other levels of meaning; indeed it does so more forcibly than the great majority of contemporary music. So, having traced important elements of Andriessen's musical design, it is time to turn to the other considerations that affect our understanding of this music. These form the basis of the following chapter.

Chapter 4

De Staat: Some Interpretations

In his review of the Amsterdam premiere of *De Staat*,[1] Elmer Schönberger noted that the piece posed a problem for anyone wishing to account for its impact. The 'impressionistic prose' often resorted to in the wake of a powerful musical experience would be entirely at odds with 'this iron-strong composition, in which the slightest impulse towards musical haziness is systematically cut short' (Schönberger 1976). Yet, as I noted in the last chapter, the work engages with such a range of ideas and preoccupations that a purely factual survey of its compositional structure is more than usually inadequate. In this chapter, I address some of these ideas and preoccupations. Specifically, I look in turn at three distinct topics. First, I examine the relation of Andriessen's work to the Plato text from which it borrows extracts and its title. Second, I assess the degree to which *De Staat* is 'about' other music, and what attitude it takes to that music. Third, I look at *De Staat* as a contribution to Andriessen's ongoing concern with the politics of musical performance. Each of these topics potentially opens up complexities of interpretation that could occupy whole chapters, if not separate monographs. Only an introduction can be offered here – although, with Schönberger's warning in mind, this limitation of space perhaps acts as a welcome constraint on hazy discursiveness. Nevertheless, *De Staat*'s idiosyncratic treatment of its set text, of its 'intertextual' references, and of the traditions of the concert hall, deserve careful consideration, for these things are in no small part responsible for the individual place it holds in recent musical history.

De Staat and the *Republic*

In the previous chapter I noted that *De Staat* avoids a directly illustrative response to Plato's discussion of musical modes and instruments in the *Republic*. While Andriessen was clearly interested in the topic of modes, he

---

[1] The very first performance was two days earlier (26 November 1976) in Groningen.

did not (for instance) attempt any kind of pictorial rendering of the musical characters of different modes as described by Plato. This throws open the wider question of the significance of Plato's text for *De Staat*. Andriessen's intentions seem riven with paradoxes. On the one hand, given his strong political and social commitments at the time of *De Staat*, it is little surprise that Plato's controversial account of the relation of music and society should have been of interest. On the other hand, the incorporated extracts from the *Republic* hardly hold a position of unchallenged ascendancy. *De Staat* is a predominantly instrumental work: the vocal episodes take up less than a quarter of the work's total duration. And Andriessen's distinctive approach to text-setting, which largely avoids responsiveness to the detail of the text, combined with his retention of the original Greek language, presents a huge obstacle to ready comprehensibility. Andriessen was not wholly insensitive to either the structure or the local meaning of Plato's text, and his text-setting deserves further consideration. But if we are fully to understand the significance of the *Republic* for *De Staat*, we need also to explore, first, the basis for Andriessen's reluctance to accord the text an easy prominence, and second, other levels at which the piece can be seen as responding to Plato's discourse.

Andriessen sets four extracts from the *Republic*; the second and third are longer than the others, and are combined to form the long central choral section of *De Staat*.[2] He sets the texts unaltered, retaining the generally brief interjections of Socrates' interlocutor Glaucon, and even the characteristic 'ephê' and 'ê d'hos' (both translated as 'he said') with which Plato distinguishes Glaucon's remarks. The first and second choral sections retain an element of the conversational flavour of the text by giving many of Glaucon's shorter comments, or simply the word 'ephê', to just two of the four voices.[3] Generally, though, all four voices deliver the text together, either in rhythmic unison or close imitation. This uniformity of approach extends to other aspects of the vocal parts. Andriessen's settings are unusually restrictive both rhythmically (favouring single note values or, in the second choral section, quavers and crotchets) and melodically (typically involving a handful of pitches inhabiting a narrow register). There is admittedly a certain appropriateness to this unvaried style in the outer choral sections. In the first the steady rehearsal of a Mixolydian tetrachord corresponds to the text's references to 'one musical mode' and 'similarly unchanging rhythm'. Likewise, in the final

---

[2] See Appendix A for an English translation of the full text of *De Staat*.

[3] See bars 153, 586, 601, 624 etc.; at bar 684 Glaucon is represented by just a single voice.

choral section Socrates' stern warning that 'any alteration in the modes of music is always followed by alteration in the most fundamental laws of the state' is set in an unrelievedly admonishing manner: as Andriessen describes it, 'here something important is being said' (in Desmedt 1988, p. 220). Only in the central choral section, however, does he observe the accentuation of the original Greek.[4] This section contains other modest concessions to the detail of the text. For instance, two of Socrates' inquisitorial questions about the modes are underlined by crescendos and sustained notes (bb. 619 and 649). When he turns his attention from the modes towards musical instruments, new pitches and a more cohesive choral unison are introduced (b. 668). And there are a handful of isolated instances of word-painting:[5] at bar 630 'aphajreteaj' (translated by Arnold van Akkeren as *verwerpen*, meaning 'reject' or 'condemn') is delivered in crotchet quintuplets, breaking with the predominating quavers and crotchets; 'poluharmonia' ('all modes', b. 682) and 'polukhordotaton' ('many-stringed', b. 690) receive four- and three-part settings that provide brief contrast to the stark unison that predominates in this passage; and at bar 696 the mention of the 'kithara' (a lyre) prompts the guitars to jump out of the texture with a single treble-forte unison D.

The general lack of differentiation in Andriessen's settings remains their most striking characteristic, however. It has a number of possible sources. The minimalist tendencies of *De Staat* naturally partly determined that the vocal settings would assume an economical and repetitive character. Some of Stravinsky's choral works also provided a model for the vocal writing in both *Il Principe* and *De Staat*, as mentioned in Chapter 2. Possibly the most important precedent for the approach to text-setting in *De Staat*, though, was the 'new sort of speech-song style' (Andriessen, in Koopmans 1982, p. 12) that Andriessen developed in his music for the Amsterdam Theatre School production of Brecht's *Die Massnahme* (in Dutch, *De Maatregel*) in 1972. This style was devised principally around the needs of the production's untrained singers. But it also possessed an 'agitatory' quality that was wholly in keeping with the didactic function of Brecht's Lehrstück. As Andriessen made clear in an essay on his music for the production, this agitatory quality had already been present in Hanns Eisler's original music:

> In general my melodies contain no large intervals. They are almost entirely syllabic. As for the *manner* of singing, what Eisler already wrote about the

---

[4] The sketches for *De Staat* include a typescript of the full Plato text in transliterated Greek with detailed metric annotations provided by Arnold van Akkeren.

[5] Some of these are identified in Desmedt 1988, p. 200.

singing style for his music applies in even stronger measure: unsentimental, un-aesthetic. In my music, in contrast to Eisler, even changes of dynamic are omitted: everything is loud [*hard*]. (Andriessen 1975, p. 432)

Andriessen took as his point of departure a number of Eisler's own choral movements, which comprise an unpitched, rhythmicized chant, sparely accompanied by a snare-drum pulse. In Andriessen's settings, 'the metre springs from the number of syllables, together with the shortest possible pauses between the sentences, in order to strengthen the music's agitatory character'. Textual repetition and melisma are completely avoided. The idea is that the sung text should come close to an 'agitatory *spoken* text' (ibid., pp. 437, 439).

Andriessen pursued this interest in agitatory speech in a number of other works in the early seventies. *Dat gebeurt in Vietnam* ('That happens in Vietnam') (1972), for instance, is a setting of a vivid text by Paul Binnerts – Andriessen's collaborator on the Brecht production – which adopts the changing metres and close intervals used in *De Maatregel*, but embeds them in jazzy scoring for the Orkest De Volharding. *Dat gebeurt*'s flamboyance is completely absent from *Thanh Hoa* for voice and piano (1972), which is based on a Vietnamese child's account of the bombing of her village.[6] In this short piece, the vocal line encompasses only three adjacent pitches, and the music's constantly changing metre is underlined by a bleak succession of four nervously permutated chords. *Il Principe* is a more ambitious exploration of the same principle and, as we saw in Chapter 2, it directly foreshadows the central choral section of *De Staat* in both its vocal style and aspects of its instrumental writing. Indeed, all of the vocal sections in *De Staat*, with their direct, reductive style, bear the influence of this 'agitatory' style of text-setting, establishing a direct line of continuity with the concerns and imperatives surrounding Andriessen's work on Brecht's Lehrstück.

There is, however, a peculiar conflict of intentions here. In *De Maatregel* the agitatory vocal style aims to place the text centre stage: the musical setting is intended to heighten its message. Andriessen's article on his music for the Brecht production goes out of its way to stress the importance of this, and criticizes 'American electronic avant-garde music' for using speech but not allowing it to remain intelligible (Andriessen 1975, p. 439). Yet, as has already been noted, in *De Staat* he seems decidedly ambiguous about the role of the Plato text. Not only does he retain the original ancient Greek, but the voices

---

[6] *Thanh Hoa* is contained in the volume 'The Memory of Roses' (Amsterdam: Donemus, 1999).

are pitted against a large and very noisy ensemble – a sharp contrast to the spare piano accompaniment of *De Maatregel*. And the careful adherence to the rhythmic structure of Plato's text in the central choral section is undermined by allowing the two pairs of voices to slip out of phase with each other, which results in tangled verbal canons for much of the first half of the section. The agitatory character is maintained, but Plato's message is almost totally obscured.

What explains this state of affairs? One answer is that *De Staat* relates as much to long-established preoccupations of Andriessen regarding text-setting as it does to the more recent interest in speech-song. As early as *Nocturnen* (1958) he had written for a soprano solo as if it were an orchestral instrument: the soprano sings a text, but the lyrics 'do not have any literary meaning' and they are not intended to be audible to the listener.[7] This interest in unusual musical treatments of texts was of course shared with Andriessen's teacher Berio, whose music takes all manner of approaches to literary texts. Berio's *Circles* (1960), for instance, focuses attention on the phonetic qualities of e. e. cummings's texts; and *Passaggio* (1962) highlights the non-semantic qualities of words by juxtaposing a number of different languages. Berio's *Sinfonia* (1969) provides a particular model for the treatment of the voices in *De Staat*. In *Sinfonia*, the six amplified vocalists are treated on a par with the instrumentalists: the preface to the score instructs that they 'should never overpower the orchestra' but are instead 'a vocal group amongst instrumental groups, NOT ACCOMPANIED by an orchestra'.[8]

De Staat was only the first in a series of large works by Andriessen that give a central role to a sung text, yet sets it in such a way that it is to all intents and purposes unintelligible. Bakunin's Russian, Augustine's Latin and the sixteenth-century Dutch 'Act of Abjuration' receive this kind of treatment in (respectively) *Mausoleum* (1979), *De Tijd* (1981) and Part One of *De Materie* (1987). It was an approach that chimed with Andriessen's general belief (discussed in Chapter 2) that music was incapable of expressing non-musical content. A few years after completing *De Staat*, he voiced doubts about the extent to which the music was ever intended to connect meaningfully with the Plato text. Declaring that 'music has many qualities, but not the quality of providing an equivalent to a specific text', he argued that if one wants to understand *De Staat*, 'the choice of Plato is really not so important' (Andriessen, in De Beer 1981). In this regard, there was a distinction to be made with the more explicitly 'agitatory' music of the early seventies: 'If the

---

[7] Programme note to *Nocturnen* (Muziekgroep Nederland archive).

[8] Composer's preface to the score of *Sinfonia*.

literary, as opposed to the musical, message requires direct communication, I would not dream of doing it in Greek or Russian' (Andriessen 1978, p. 49). In other words, the political impact of a work like *De Staat* resided not with the text, but with the more exclusively musical matters of instrumentation and performance style.

One should be wary of allowing these later opinions wholly to determine our understanding of the piece. The published score makes it quite clear that the audience must be provided with a copy of the Plato text, which would hardly appear to be congruent with the idea that it was unimportant. And there remains a level at which Andriessen's distinctive treatment of his text in *De Staat* is, after all, consistent with the goals of the Brechtian Lehrstück. As he states in the note accompanying the first recording of *De Staat*, he incorporates Plato's text, not to endorse it, but to hold it up for critical scrutiny. This approach unifies all three works in the political trilogy of which *De Staat* is a part – the others being *Il Duce* and *Il Principe*. Andriessen claims that, in each of these pieces, 'my efforts are concentrated on providing a musical and rhetorical *commentary* on the highly disputable views contained in the text' (Andriessen 1977b, p. 43). The model was explicitly that of the Lehrstück which, in the words of Brecht, 'aims to show incorrect political attitudes and thus to teach correct ones' (Brecht 1997, pp. 232–33):

> *Il Duce* and *Il Principe* … are in the tradition of Bertolt Brecht. I would say that, like Brecht in his plays, I have developed anti- or negative-social models as a special kind of epic theatre. *Il Duce* uses a text by Mussolini, *Il Principe* a text by Machiavelli, and those are examples, I believe, of how one should not act politically. That is a Brechtian way of composing. (Andriessen, in Gronemeyer 1992, p. 55)

In the case of *De Staat*, it is Plato's 'Stalinist views about the function of music' (Andriessen, in Kimberley 1994, p. 38) that qualified his text for this treatment, and specifically his proposal that music that has effects undesirable to the state should be suppressed. *De Staat* is different from the earlier pieces in the trilogy, though, in that Andriessen felt a measure of ambivalence towards the text as a whole. At the time of the premiere he referred to a 'love-hate' relationship, one caused by the fact that, despite the repressive implications of what Plato has to say, he at least 'attached tremendous value to music and the influence it had on people' (Andriessen, in Reichenfeld 1976). As he later commented, 'if only it were true that musical innovation represented a danger to the State!' (Andriessen 1977b, p. 43). But this ambivalent attitude towards the Plato text, far from detracting from *De Staat*'s functioning as a Lehrstück, is in fact consistent with it. For it was not Brecht's intention that a Lehrstück should, in the words of Douglas Kellner, set forth 'correct doctrine'. Rather, the aim was to set out a complex situation for which a solution would be found only through the process of discussion between participants and audience, a process that was an intrinsic part of the whole concept (Kellner 1997). In other words, the Lehrstück aimed to stimulate thought about its content, not to provide easy answers.

The principal difficulty in viewing *De Staat* in terms of the Brechtian Lehrstück, then, is the way in which much of Plato's text is rendered inaudible. Andriessen's setting resolutely ignores Eisler's requirement in relation to *Die Massnahme*, surely fundamental to the genre if its didactic function is to be realized, that 'the whole audience must be able to understand the text throughout' (Eisler, in Brecht 1997, p. 234). However, compromising the intelligibility of a text, while at odds with the principle of the Lehrstück, remains an effectively direct way of declaring one's opposition to it; certainly in *De Staat* tensions between text and music are consistent with, rather than contrary to, the reason for including the text in the first place. It is possible, too, to discern behind this antagonistic approach the influence of a different element of Brecht's theory of theatre, namely the idea of 'the separation of the elements' (Brecht 1964, p. 37). This idea, which proposed that the diverse components of a texted musical work, instead of striving for unanimity, should retain their independence and thus their ability to comment on each other, was central to Brecht's theory of epic theatre. It was intended as an antidote to the fusion of the Wagnerian *Gesamtkunstwerk*, which promoted only 'hypnosis' and 'sordid intoxication' – and thus worked against the detached reflection that was the proper aim of the modern theatre (Brecht 1964, pp. 37–38). Andriessen has often described the music of *De Staat* as 'angry', even 'furious and hysterical' (see for instance De Vries 1976), and this anger is at least in part directed specifically towards the Plato text. Thus, the harshly strident setting of the final Plato extract highlights the repressive connotations of Socrates' warning against altering music. The 'jackboot stomp' (Wright 1993, p. 10) following the central choral section likewise acts as an expression of horror at Socrates' intention of 'purging the city' which had grown 'too luxurious' – a threat that might have particular resonance for an Amsterdamer. The obscuring of textual meaning at the start of this long choral section should also be viewed from this perspective. In Andriessen's setting, the naive details of Plato's discussion of modes and instruments are not allowed to detract from the real issue, which is the dictatorial tendencies of authority – tendencies of which the so-called 'agitatory' vocal style is itself sufficiently expressive.

Comparisons with Brecht and the Lehrstück, and the existence of such dramatic internal tensions between music and text, point to a general affinity between *De Staat* and theatre. This is hardly surprising. As we saw in Chapter 1, Andriessen was involved in a number of theatre productions during the period of *De Staat*'s composition, and its first performance followed hard on the heels of the first of three music-theatre works that he wrote for the Baal theatre company. In recent years Andriessen has gone further in making the connection: 'I wait for the moment when *De Staat* and *De Tijd* provide the basis for a full-evening theater performance by a great choreographer or director.... These pieces are theater works more than anything else' (in Trochimczyk (ed.) 2002, p. 230).[9] In performance, *De Staat* has never been accompanied by the elaborate staging that marked the premiere of *De Tijd* in 1981, for instance, with its light projections and mechanical representations of time (see Potter 1981, p. 21). But film clips of the 1978 revival of *De Staat* show a marked attentiveness to the visual impact of the performance, with the four singers raised high against a lit backdrop at the back of the Carré Theatre stage, and the performers informally dressed.[10] The 1994 edition of the score (published by Boosey and Hawkes) additionally requests that the performers should stand, Volharding-style.

A blurring of the boundaries between music and theatre characterized other Dutch music in the late sixties and seventies, not least that of Andriessen's erstwhile collaborators Misha Mengelberg and Willem Breuker. From early in its existence, performances by the Instant Composers Pool were moulded into surreal dramas complete with costumes and scenery (Koopmans 1977); and Mengelberg's and Breuker's later independent work similarly merged musical and theatrical performance (Whitehead 1999, pp. 83–84, 91–92, 105). Andriessen has never been as experimental on this front: none of his instrumental works demand the stage movement or theatrical gestures required in works by Berio and Birtwistle, for instance. Nevertheless, *De Staat* contains a strong element of instrumental theatre simply by virtue of the marked way in which different performers form allegiances and oppositions. Two elements of his scoring are particularly significant in this respect: unison, and antiphonal interplay between the two halves of the ensemble. Andriessen's relative lack of concern for the audibility of his text is partly compensated for by these instrumental interactions, which offer symbolic resonances with many of the issues raised by Plato.

Andriessen has described unison as the central concern of all his music

---

[9] See also Andriessen 2002, p. 42.

[10] Clips were included in the film 'Domein van de Vrijheid', directed by Ad 's Gravesande and Sieuwert Verster and broadcast on Dutch television on 26 June 1996.

between 1970 and 1977.[11] The appeal of unison textures was partly that they had been a taboo of the post-war avant-garde – being deemed a superfluous, essentially colouristic device. But they also offered an obvious musical metaphor for political solidarity and equality. *De Staat*'s 'philosophy of democracy', as Andriessen has termed it – which is to say, the idea that every part is as important as the others (see Andriessen 1990b, p. 150) – clearly chimed with this politicized conception. And yet it is significant that *De Staat*, like *Melodie* (1974), in which the close doubling of the two instruments is prone to occasional 'derailment' (Andriessen and Schönberger 1979, p. 16), is as much about the 'failed unison'[12] as about perfect unanimity. Even when the voices are proclaiming in the first choral section the merits of song uttered in a 'uniform character', their vocal line frays periodically, the two pairs of voices briefly parting company to create fibrous dissonances. In this way they anticipate the knottier canonic polyphony of the central choral section. Elsewhere, unisons are dislocated into canons, or made so difficult to play that an exact alliance is rendered impossible.

The division of the ensemble into two equal halves is one of the principal threats to unison in *De Staat*. The two sub-ensembles are visually articulated by the strictly symmetrical layout of the musicians on the stage, and their clearest musical manifestation is at the end of the work, where the left side of the ensemble engages the right in a furious canon. The interaction between the two halves of the ensemble provides *De Staat*'s principal means of engaging symbolically with the broader issues of social divisiveness and control raised by Plato's text. There is a distinct evolution in this relationship as the piece proceeds. Initially, homogeneous textures, to which each half of the ensemble contributes equally, prevail; it is the different instrumental families, rather than left and right, that are pitted against each other at the very start of the work. The bipartite division comes to the fore only briefly in the first half of the piece: first, in the unison semiquaver melodies, where the oboe and trumpet parts are distributed between the pairs of instrumentalists on either side; and second, more ominously, at bar 349, where left and right ensembles snarl aggressively at each other. It is at the start of the central choral section that the division becomes a major concern. As I noted above, the four voices here fail to maintain a precise unison and split into two out-of-sync pairs, and each pair of voices is doubled by one half of the ensemble (minus brass and violas). Thus it is that Socrates' injunctions on which music must be abolished directly

---

[11] In 1977 he wrote that, 'since 1970 my pieces form one story which is about unison' (Andriessen 1977a, p. 141).

[12] On the failed unison, see Andriessen 1997/1999b, pp. 274–76.

prompt the first major fracture of the ensemble into left and right. The division remains significant throughout the remainder of the work. From bar 791, for instance, each half of the ensemble jostles for control of the downbeat, the music's shifting barlines adding to the instability of the situation (see Ex. 4.1). The hocketing melody that follows shortly afterwards (b. 893) – significant (as we saw in the last chapter) as the work's first complete and unfettered statement of the diatonic scale – is in fact made up of two independent melodies played by either half of the ensemble. For much of this section these manage to cooperate: the successive notes of the two melodies smoothly alternate to provide the illusion of a single, slightly blurred line. But towards the end the effort to maintain a corporate front proves too great and the schism in the ensemble becomes impossible to ignore (see Ex. 4.2).

It is left to the spectacular closing canon, which follows in the wake of the final Plato extract, to try to resolve the conflict (see Ex. 4.3). The right-hand side of the ensemble initially trails the left by a duration of three crotchets, but it is also prone to wander from the original subject. On the first occasion that it strays in this way, it causes the canon to stutter to a near halt (b. 958). On

Ex. 4.1   *De Staat*: **antiphonal hocket at bb. 797–822 (left and right ensembles, omitting oboes and trumpets)**

Ex. 4.2 *De Staat*: **hocketing melody (left and right ensembles) at bb. 910–22**

the second occasion, the music appears more determined to keep going (a crescendo and 'tutta forza' marking accompany the demise of the canon at b. 983), and the music transforms into a fitful hocket, the time delay between the two parts suddenly dissolved. Pauses and continual shifts in speed symbolize the effort required to achieve, firstly, a rhythmic unison, and then, finally (seven bars before the end), full pitch unison. This is the only literal unison involving the whole ensemble in *De Staat*, and its hard-won arrival is regarded by the composer as 'the major subject of the work' (Andriessen 1977b, p. 43).

Thus the instrumental drama enacted in *De Staat* serves to underline Andriessen's critical, Brechtian view of Plato's text. The struggle to achieve and maintain musical unanimity is one waged against the divisive sentiments of the text – popular solidarity being the necessary response to the quashing of musical freedom. The unison achieved at the very end of the piece is too briefly glimpsed to allow any complacency about the 'victory' of the music over the text. But it follows that individual freedom and diversity are seen as the goal of solidarity: that, in other words, the need for everyone to act identically is a means rather than an end. In the next section I will develop this idea with the suggestion that it is the more elaborate textures of the second of the long, diatonic homages to American minimalism, rather than the grim unison of the end, that *De Staat* presents as its utopia. This interpretation

Ex. 4.3 *De Staat*: final part of antiphonal canon (left and right ensembles), b. 979 to end

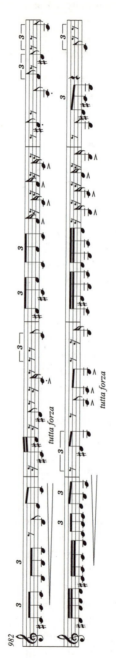

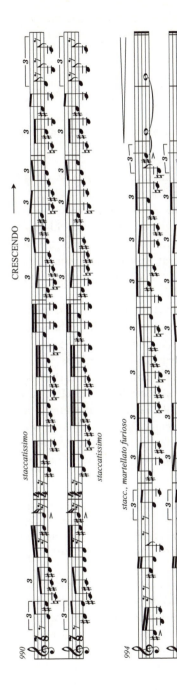

depends on a stance regarding Andriessen's attitude to other musics – an examination of which will also throw light on other aspects of *De Staat*'s meaning.

Music about Music

> All good music is about other music. (Andriessen, in Van Rossum and Smit 1994, p. 15)

As we saw in Chapter 2, Andriessen regards composition as an act of engagement with existing musical styles, rather than an opportunity for strictly personal expression. As a result, his music frequently makes identifiable reference to other music. One can see this throughout his oeuvre: in the diverse idioms explored in his earliest works, the polystylistic music of the late sixties, the engagement with jazz and American minimalism in the seventies, and the moments of pastiche and quotation in the stage works from the nineties.

Andriessen would see this aspect of his music as consistent with a Stravinskian outlook on composition, and more broadly with a 'classicist' aesthetic. But such stylistic pluralism – the 'anti-purist versatility' to which Elmer Schönberger has referred (Schönberger 2001, p. 637) – also aligns him with postmodernism. Andriessen himself is less than enthusiastic about being considered a postmodernist composer. Yayoi Uno Everett has written that for Andriessen the term 'implies the reduction of art to pastiche, nostalgia, and late-capitalistic modes of commodification' (Everett, forthcoming). This is perhaps predictable, in so far as the apparent relativism fostered by postmodernist thought is at odds with his strongly held political convictions. In 1997 he recalled that:

> At the beginning of the eighties, someone confessed to me that he didn't know what postmodernism was. I said, I don't really know that well either, but I think that it means that Marx is out and Nietzsche is in. I still believe that that is a good description of what was going on. (Andriessen 1997/1999b, p. 276)

Nevertheless, definitions of musical postmodernism have clear relevance for Andriessen's music in that they typically highlight the importance of explicit references to other musical styles – styles drawn either from previous historical eras, or from popular and non-Western musics. More generally, postmodern music is seen as foregrounding the way in which any form of individual expression, however authentic and unique it may seem, is at root a negotiation of the forms and practices to hand in culture.[13] As modern culture makes available an increasingly broad palette of identities and behaviours, so the ways in which individuals express themselves become more diverse and unpredictable. Thus, in place of the modernist insistence that the evolution of history demands a similarly progressive approach to musical style – that, in other words, musical style must follow an unerring, single path of development in order to be adequate to the times – style becomes simply a matter of personal choice. Postmodernist composers face a range of options. A single, relatively coherent style may be adopted from history. Or, alternatively, many different styles can be playfully juxtaposed. Many postmodern composers take paths somewhere in between these two extremes. Different attitudes may also be taken towards the adopted styles: they can be endorsed, celebrated, critiqued or parodied. One can trace a line of development in this respect in Andriessen's own handling of other music. *Anachronie I* and *Reconstructie*, for instance, seem to take a neutral stance towards their quotations and style citations. Here the references are intended more as a 'vulgar' rebuke of avant-garde purism than as comment on the sources themselves. In *Rosa* and *Writing to Vermeer*, on the other hand, Andriessen's warm evocations of film music and Baroque dances suggest a far more immediate identification on the part of the composer with the adopted styles; in these and other recent works, he takes pleasure in displaying his wide-ranging musical enthusiasms.

Separating these two periods, however, was a phase in which references to other music were intended to serve a quite different function: that of critique. As we saw in Chapter 1, the idea of critique was a central principle for the Orkest De Volharding. De Volharding's repertoire took the 'music of the people' as its point of departure, but it was also intent on challenging and developing existing musical tastes. Andriessen's music during this period reflects this. *Dat gebeurt in Vietnam*, for instance, embeds its strongly anti-American text in 'a kind of parody of big-band music' (Andriessen, in Whitehead 1999, p. 79): the familiar musical idiom is thus cast in a critical light. Similarly, *On Jimmy Yancey* quotes some Yancey tunes only for them to stop mid-flow, with the effect (in the mind of the composer) that they become 'alienated' (Andriessen, in Witts 1978, p. 10). The same principle extended to the Amsterdam Theatre School production of *De Maatregel*: Andriessen's music 'originated in musical conventions familiar to the members of the group [of performers], but these conventions were criticized and moved beyond'

---

[13] Accessible literature on this topic includes Hartwell 1993 and Lochhead and Auner (eds) 2002.

(Andriessen 1975, p. 433). In this respect, he viewed Eisler's original music for *Die Massnahme* as providing a model: the use of 'progressive means' to 'criticize and develop the musical reference points of the producers' was a strategy borrowed directly from Eisler (pp. 431–32). Thus, Eisler's 'Prelude' clearly refers to the opening of Bach's *St Matthew Passion*, but for Andriessen it does so 'not as a tribute, but as critique'. Similarly, the song of the 'despicable capitalist' rice merchant takes the form of a tango, a satirical reference that built on Eisler's view that 'light music under capitalism is ... a dangerous poison for the masses' (pp. 431, 442–43).

Is the same critical attitude towards referenced styles evident in *De Staat*? The idea of critique is very evidently in operation in relation to the Plato text, as discussed earlier in this chapter: the text is incorporated in order to expose its weaknesses. But the tendency to group *De Staat* with the substantial works on philosophical topics written in the following years (such as the stylistically homogeneous *De Tijd* (1981) and *De Snelheid* (1984)) has encouraged a rather monolithic view of the work:[14] its divergent influences are acknowledged, but these are assumed to be assimilated into a coherent personal language. It is only by viewing *De Staat* in the context of the citation works of the late sixties and the critical attitude of the Volharding years that it becomes easier to see it as a continuation of a long-term concern with references to other musics. As noted in Chapter 3, minimalism, Berio, gamelan and (more subtly) Stravinsky all make an appearance. I suggested there that the work's more chromatic materials act in particular as a form of critique of the blander diatonicism of American minimalism against which they are so harshly juxtaposed. There are other reasons for seeing *De Staat* as, in the words of John Pickard, a 'fierce critique' of minimalism (Pickard 1994, p. 57) – and thus a direct extension of the preoccupation with critique of the Volharding period. It was noted in Chapter 2 how, during the last year of work on *De Staat*, Andriessen was being prompted to take a more critical view of minimalism by some of the students with whom he was working on the Hoketus project. The desire to 'roughen it up, damage the goods' (Whitehead 1999, p. 61) was of course already an aspect of Andriessen's first minimalistic exercise, *De Volharding*: from the start, American minimalism seemed too innocuous to represent a decisive break with bourgeois music culture. As we saw in Chapter 3, though, *De Staat* is different from either *De Volharding* or *Hoketus* in making such direct and 'authentic' reference to American minimalism in the first half of the piece – only starkly to juxtapose it against material that is in important respects its opposite. Is it the case, then, that in the wake of Philip Glass's successful

---

[14] See e.g. Schönberger 1998 and Wright 1993.

performances around the Netherlands in 1975, *De Staat* was, precisely in the manner of De Volharding, taking the then current tastes of the progressive concert audience, and subjecting them to unsparingly critical scrutiny?

To answer this effectively, we need a fuller appreciation of the specifically *musical* consequences of Andriessen's attitudes at this time – for they do not always correspond to his spoken statements. It is rare, for instance, for his music obviously to satirize other music, in the way that Eisler does in his archly witty tango in *Die Massnahme*.[15] (It is significant in this regard that Andriessen encountered some difficulty in identifying an appropriate way to replicate this satirical effect in his own musical setting of the same number; Andriessen 1975, p. 443.) There are a few exceptions, as we have already seen in this book: the 'pop' arrangement (complete with flattened sevenths) of the 'Ode to Joy' in *The Nine Symphonies of Beethoven* brings this most 'elevated' of works crashing down to earth; and *Il Duce* pits the inflated strains of Richard Strauss against Mussolini's voice, to pointed effect. Elsewhere, though, Andriessen's references are free of caricature or exaggeration, and indeed often seem notably affectionate. This is true as early as the *Souvenirs d'enfance*, the knowing irony of the written preface notwithstanding:[16] each piece is a successful exercise in pastiche and makes no attempt to derail the chosen style with pointed gestures of any kind.

As Andriessen made clear in his essay on his citation works in *De Gids*, the effort to 'make all areas of music contemporary' rendered the concept of 'parody' out of date and redundant (Andriessen 1968d, p. 179). This is in sharp contrast to contemporaries such as Peter Maxwell Davies or Mauricio Kagel, for instance, whose references to popular or historical styles were often satirical in intention – a manifestation, in essence, of the hostility towards mass culture common to much modernist endeavour.[17] For Andriessen, the model of Ives dictated that all music should be embraced, 'without caricature' (ibid.). *Anachronie I*, therefore, makes a point of showcasing the vulgar

---

[15] Albrecht Betz describes this tango as a 'wicked parody' (Betz 1982, p. 100). Even without the politicized dramatic context, the tango's exaggerated dynamics and tempo changes mark it out as a 'send up'.

[16] According to the preface to *Souvenirs d'enfance*, the 'Sonatensatz' is an 'example of How Not to Compose'; the 'Nocturne' in the style of Fauré is 'a sweet for madam, and for Alex van Amerongen' (a conservative music critic); and the serial 'Ricercare' is 'to be studied and analysed'.

[17] On this point see Steve Sweeney-Turner, 'Resurrecting the Antichrist: Maxwell Davies and parody – dialectics or deconstruction?', *Tempo*, **191** (Winter 1994), 17 n. 17. On parody in Kagel see Paul Attinello, 'Imploding the system: Kagel and the deconstruction of modernism', in Lochhead and Auner (eds) 2002, pp. 263–86.

alongside the refined, but never descends into point-scoring or nose-thumbing: Michel Legrand and Messiaen exist happily side by side. The possibility that one might treat something as tasteless *and* admire it at the same time is the major theme of Andriessen's 1966 essay on camp (Andriessen 1966; see especially pp. 54–55).

By 1971 Andriessen's aesthetic priorities had undergone considerable change, as we saw in Chapter 1. But his *music* continued to demonstrate a conviction in the validity of popular or familiar musical styles – even when his political standpoint and spoken statements would seem to make such neutrality over popular musical material impossible. During 1971, at the very time the philosophy behind the Orkest De Volharding was being formulated, Andriessen was adding the finishing touches to *Le Voile du bonheur* for violin and piano (1966/71). This short piece juxtaposes a perfumed, early twentieth-century salon style with a 1960s pop song, sung by the violinist. A kind of untranslatable Dutch irony may be at work here – the combination of severity and silliness that Andriessen so loves in Mondrian (see Trochimczyk (ed.) 2002, p. 69), and which was also the prime characteristic of the Dutch social protests of the 1960s. But this ironic attitude notwithstanding, both styles are presented with complete conviction, entirely free of caricature. Additionally, the eventual resumption of the salon piece at the end balances the initially deflating impact of the pop song, so that neither style seems to occupy the critical 'high ground'.

Andriessen continued to turn his hand to varied historical or popular idioms during the seventies. The two works adjacent to *De Staat* in Donemus's official worklist give an indication of the irreducible plurality of his compositional style at the time. *Monuments of the Netherlands* for wind band (1975)[18] is a sturdy, stylistically conservative showpiece (in A minor) that is not afraid to indulge in clichéd marching rhythms, wind trills and drum rolls. The musical numbers of *Matthew Passion* (1976), meanwhile, are unsurprisingly saturated with references to the forms and musical style of the Bach Passions: the idiom is updated, of course, but only to the extent that the music sometimes sounds more like a faithful pastiche of Stravinsky than it does of Bach. In recent years Andriessen has made a distinction between his 'official' works intended for the concert hall, and 'instant music' written for friends, film or the theatre (Andriessen 1998b, p. 245); there is little doubt that he would assign *Monuments* and *Matthew Passion* (not to mention *Le Voile du bonheur*) to the latter category. But this does not affect the fact that these

---

[18] The work also has a Dutch title, *Nederland, let op Uw Schoonheyt* ['Netherlands, attend to your beauty'].

pieces are testament to the diversity of his musical predilections, and his willingness to indulge those enthusiasms in his own compositions.

Even in the Volharding pieces, where a critical attitude towards common musical tastes is supposed to be to the fore, one senses a tension between Andriessen's social-political convictions and his musical instincts. In *Dat gebeurt in Vietnam* and *On Jimmy Yancey*, 'critique' can be difficult to distinguish from 'love', for the adopted styles are wielded with great relish and without any of the distancing strategies that might encourage a more critical view. This is not simply a matter of the absence of a satirical attitude, but of any factor that might encourage us to view the referenced music as 'objectified', or 'presented as "represented"' (Heile 2002, p. 289) – which is to say, distinct from the prevailing authorial voice. One might say the same of the earlier twentieth-century works that Andriessen held up as exemplifications of the 'critical' attitude: both Milhaud's *La Création du monde* and Stravinsky's *Tango* enthusiastically incorporate and build upon their popular sources, rather than treat them as practices that need 'criticizing' and 'moving beyond'. Indeed, the most obviously 'critical' gesture in Andriessen's *On Jimmy Yancey*, far from being directed against the boogie-woogie source, actually springs from it: the chirpy little cadence that ends both movements, which is based on Yancey's own characteristic closing lick, effectively punctures the ardent portentousness of the immediately preceding music. It is as if Yancey himself is wagging his own finger at the earnest socio-musical aspirations of the young Dutch composer.

At root, Andriessen's compositional attitude to pre-existing music is as much determined by the '"take, eat" attitude' of Stravinsky[19] as it is by considerations of alienation and critique, however important the latter were for the manifestos and spoken statements of the Volharding years. In *The Apollonian Clockwork*, the authors quote from Stravinsky: 'I can follow only where my musical appetites lead me.... Whatever interests me, whatever I love, I wish to make my own' (in Andriessen and Schönberger 1989, pp. 104–5). The same motivation – the alighting upon a musical model because it pleases him – underlies all Andriessen's negotiations with other music.[20] And the consequence may be that, for Andriessen as much as for Stravinsky, the 'distinction commonly made between "arrangements" and

---

[19] The quotation is from Robin Holloway, 'Modernism and after', in Peter Davison (ed.), *Reviving the Muse: Essays on Music after Modernism* (Brinkworth, Wiltshire: Claridge Press, 2001), p. 102.

[20] In recent years Andriessen has been more open about this: 'The basic reason you deal with certain musical material is because you love it' (in Whitehead 1999, p. 241).

"original compositions" is not pertinent' (ibid., p. xiii). Once a composer's personal musical sympathies range so widely and the composer has the inclination to reflect those sympathies in his or her own music, musical borrowing tends to merge into original composition. This situation is hardly conducive to the detachment necessary for a genuinely critical view of pre-existing musical forms. If this seems to contradict Andriessen's stated principles on the matter, it is nevertheless consistent with his longer-held conviction that musical material does not possess anything other than a strictly musical meaning. Under this view the expressive or ideological content that people hear in music springs from habitual, arbitrary associations, or the circumstances of performance, not the notes themselves. This has the congenial consequence that, as different musical styles are not at root culpable of the various social meanings that become attached to them – the bourgeois connotations of turn-of-the-century salon music for instance, or the 'commodity character' of pop – they may be alluded to or borrowed with impunity, even by the politically minded composer.

This stance can be demonstrated by looking at Andriessen's original programme note to *De Staat*, and other comments he made about the work at the time of the first performances. The programme note offers a somewhat confused picture. Andriessen initially distances himself from those who view composing as 'suprasocial': music and society are thoroughly co-implicated. He continues:

> The only point on which I agree with the liberal idealists is that abstract musical material – pitch, duration and rhythm – is suprasocial: it is part of nature. There is no such thing as a fascist dominant seventh. The moment the musical material is ordered however, it becomes culture and, as such, a given social fact. (Andriessen 1977b, p. 43)

At first sight, this seems a viable stance. The most basic constituents of music are raw, 'natural' phenomena that carry no social meaning until they have been organized by a composer, played by performers and heard by listeners. The difficulty arises, however, with Andriessen's implication that 'unordered' musical material includes such things as a dominant seventh. Instead of seeing the dominant seventh as the product of a particular historical musical culture – that of eighteenth-century Europe – he treats it as a natural formation that carries no such associations.

This uncertainty about what constitutes natural, 'suprasocial' musical material and what constitutes an ordered musical idea reflects Andriessen's more general, thoroughly Stravinskian doubt that *any* music carries extra-musical meaning in and of itself. In an interview at the time of the premiere of

De Staat, Andriessen extended the realm of apolitical musical material to encompass scales:

> Certain scales were undoubtedly used a lot in cafés in Plato's time, and had an inflammatory [*opzwepend*] character, just as the music of the Rolling Stones does now. But that tells us nothing about these scales. The musical material in itself is not political; it is abstract. (In De Vries 1976)

Eighteen months later, Andriessen was pressed on the question of what constituted the political element of music in an interview with Dick Witts. Witts suggested to him that Stockhausen's music, despite its apparent 'progressiveness', had a reactionary political impact:

> LA: Yes, but you cannot analyse music in a political way. That's impossible. You can see Stockhausen's reactionary attitude in his dealings with musicians, or in his writings .... But that does not say anything about the organisation of the material, which may be of future help to music.
>
> DW: I can see how particular frequencies or durations aren't 'political'; they're natural material. But ... I can't see how organised material can be politically blank.
>
> LA: I think it is in fact, yeah. (Witts 1978, p. 9)

With this – and dismissals of social readings of compositional styles as 'playing a game' and 'vague analogies' – Andriessen flatly denied his already somewhat hesitant assertion to the contrary in the programme note to *De Staat*. The comparison between Plato and the Rolling Stones appears again in a discussion from 1979, and this time Andriessen is more unambiguous: 'I can play the entire repertoire of the Rolling Stones on the piano without a chair being damaged.... It is not the scale which causes the excitement, but the way in which it is used' (Andriessen and Schönberger 1979, p. 16). The implication here – that *De Staat*, like the Rolling Stones, is political principally on account of its attitude to performance, rather than its musical material – lurks behind all Andriessen's comments on the piece. And by placing the emphasis on performance in this way, it remained possible for him to continue admiring the *music* of Stockhausen (for instance) when other composers with a similar interest in progressive politics – notably, Cornelius Cardew – had long since rejected it.[21] Likewise, he could continue to indulge in his own dealings with

---

[21] By the early 1970s Cardew viewed the music of Stockhausen as 'a part of the cultural superstructure of the largest-scale system of human oppression and exploitation the world has ever known: imperialism' (Cardew 1974, p. 47). The

musical material that had commercial or bourgeois associations – minimalism, film music, pop – without any obligation to adopt a critical pose. The idea that one can 'read from the score, from the notes, what is socially progressive and what is not', Andriessen declares, is a 'mistake' made by 'totalitarian thinkers' (ibid., p. 16).

This reading of the role of performers and performance in determining the political meaning of *De Staat* will be pursued in the next section of this chapter. In the meantime, let us return to the question of the piece's relation to American minimalism. At one level the work presents a generous homage to Andriessen's American contemporaries. Where *Workers Union* and *Hoketus* deploy repetitive figuration but problematize it with dissonant harmony and unpredictable metric shifts, the first half of *De Staat* contains extended periods of diatonic minimalist patterns in regular 4/4 metre, moreover treated with the sort of orchestrational 'luxuriousness' that Andriessen rather guiltily enjoyed in Philip Glass (see Koopmans 1976b, p. 36). As such, it exemplifies the sort of blame-free attitude towards musical styles identified in the preceding argument. On the other hand, as I noted earlier, *De Staat*'s yoking together of the happy diatonic undulations of the American minimalists with music of bitingly dissonant ferocity hardly represents an unconditional advocacy. Now, from the point of view of someone like Theodor Adorno – the most prominent twentieth-century expositor of the idea of critique in music – Andriessen's music fails the requirements for critique several times over.[22] Not only does it incorporate stylistic references without the 'framing or distancing device' needed, from an Adornian viewpoint, 'to induce a tension between the material and its form' (Williams 1997, p. 132), but his musical idiom is also replete with all the various aspects of Stravinsky's style that, for Adorno, unerringly connoted the demise of the individual in contemporary society. These have been enumerated by Jonathan Cross:

> Mechanical repetitiveness and the fetishisation of rhythm; an identification with folklore (non-Western culture), with the collective ...; a depersonalisation and emphasis on ritual; a regressive primitivism ...; and the eradication of 'the subjective experience of time' resulting in the atomisation of musical materials. (Cross 1998, p. 234)

Defenders of Stravinsky, however, have sought to argue that his music was

---

parallels and differences between Cardew and Andriessen during the late sixties and early seventies would make for a fascinating study.

[22] One assumes in turn that Adorno is one of the 'totalitarian thinkers' to which Andriessen refers in the quotation in the previous paragraph.

'capable of registering both affiliation and resistance' to the pre-existing sources that it incorporates (Williams 1997, p. 135) – in other words, the possibility of an attitude that combines both identification *and* critique. Andriessen himself described the critical attitude of De Volharding as 'springing from involvement with what you criticise' (Andriessen 1972, p. 134), and his music is as accommodating to this kind of interpretation as Stravinsky's. One way of expressing the situation would be that the music of both Stravinsky and Andriessen avoids blatant techniques of alienation (for all that the term is bandied about in Andriessen's spoken statements during the 1970s),[23] but it remains 'dialectical'. And dialectic – understood as 'the interaction of contradictory or opposite forces' (Williams 1976, p. 92) – carries its own critical charge. Brecht will again have been influential on Andriessen in this regard. Taking a cue from the Marxist reading of human history in terms of 'a continual clash of opposing factors leading to a situation where everything was in a state of qualitative and quantitative change' (Willett 1998, p. 223), Brecht saw dialectical oppositions as crucial to 'the critical attitude' after which modern theatre must strive (Brecht 1964, p. 185). Accordingly, his theatre works strove to expose the contradictions motivating progress and history by focusing on his characters' inconsistencies, disharmony and imperfections (ibid., p. 195). In contrast to classical Hegelian dialectics (but in line with Adorno's 'negative dialectics') no attempt was made to wring a 'synthesizing progression'[24] from these oppositions: the audience must be left to reach its own conclusion.

Similarly, writers on Stravinsky have advanced the idea that, in a work like *Pulcinella*, the 'criticism of received materials' emerges dialectically – that is, from 'the centrifugal tension arising out of the confrontation of irreconcilable forces'.[25] Stravinsky would doubtless have given short shrift to such a reading. Andriessen, on the other hand, has often used the word 'dialectical' to describe his music, and to judge from a statement made in 1998, the coining of 'splendid, crackling, electrifying antitheses' (Andriessen 1998a, p. 74) remains absolutely central to his approach to composition today. *De Staat* presents countless moments of sharply drawn musical contradiction, particularly between the diatonic 'minimalist' music and its surroundings. This is not simply a matter of the harmonic clash of diatonic harmony and the

---

[23] See e.g. Witts 1978, p. 10 and Andriessen and Schönberger 1979, p. 15.

[24] I borrow the term from Alastair Williams, *Constructing Musicology* (Aldershot: Ashgate, 2001), p. 11.

[25] The quotations come from Glenn Watkins and Richard Taruskin respectively. Both are cited in Cross 1998, pp. 237–38.

rudest of chromatic dissonances. It is also a matter of juxtaposing regular metre with acute rhythmic asymmetry (as at b. 264), harmonic staticity with dizzying harmonic change (as at b. 349), and moderate dynamics and legatissimo playing with the rawest of treble *fortes* (as at b. 492). The second half of the piece, in which the style of the American minimalists is not evoked so clearly, nevertheless persists with these black-and-white oppositions. Andriessen's refusal to engineer a neat synthesis or resolution at the end of the piece leaves the matter open for public debate, just as Brecht would wish.

The idea that Andriessen is not simply hostile to American minimalism[26] – that critique, if it emerges at all, emerges dialectically rather than through wholesale repudiation – receives some confirmation if we think back to my earlier discussion of instrumental theatre. From this point of view, the sections of the work most redolent of American minimalism represent something of a utopia, for they exist independently of either the severe homophonic unisons or the divisive binary textures of the rest of the score. In particular, the long section beginning at bar 409 – an undisguised evocation, as I suggested in Chapter 3, of Riley's *In C* and Glass's *Music in Twelve Parts* – presents a kind of anarchistic collectivity in which individuals are free to make distinct contributions (such as the relaxed melodic solos from b. 445 onwards) to the harmonious impression of the whole. This textural quality is particularly striking in the light of the acrimonious antiphonal split that appears for the first time shortly before (at b. 349). Maybe this passage represents the 'soft and convivial' music that Plato wishes to suppress; the warmth of Andriessen's handling of these minimalist passages – the lack of alienatory distance – certainly makes it clear which side of the debate he is on. But the dialectical principle cannot allow such music to stand by itself; as Andriessen will have learnt from Brecht, a dreamy presentation of a utopia will only send the audience into a passive 'trance' (Brecht 1964, p. 187), unable to use their experience to effect social change. Thus it is that Andriessen juxtaposes it with music designed to establish the most tense of oppositions, oppositions that recognize the freedoms and harmony of a relaxed minimalist style to be illusory in present conditions. The more worldly, grimly industrious unison finally wrested, at the very end of the work, from these earlier antitheses is the best that can be hoped for in this light: a step towards the fuller liberation at which the music had fondly hinted, but diagnosed as far from being a reality.

---

[26] It is interesting to note in this connection that the ensemble Hoketus, for all its initial antipathy to American minimalism, had a Philip Glass commission slated for the 1980/1981 season (Hoketus publicity, Muziekgroep Nederland archive). The commission never came to fruition.

The Politics of Performance

> What I am ultimately concerned with is not only inventing new music, but
> developing new ways of playing, and contributing other (new) ways for
> musicians to deal with their instruments and with music – in other words, an
> alternative musical practice.... If you want to change music, and that is the
> composer's most important task, then you must change music-making too.
> (Andriessen 1977a, p. 141)

Those who were present at the Amsterdam premiere of *De Staat* on
28 November 1976 vividly recall the excitement it caused. The Amsterdam
Concertgebouw, in spite of its lofty history, princely interiors and
intimate association with the Concertgebouw Orchestra, was no stranger to
more unconventional musical events: it had a long history of staging jazz
concerts, for instance, and this premiere belonged to a regular series of
contemporary music concerts (the 'C-series'). Nevertheless, the raw, pop-
like energy of *De Staat*, unrelenting over 35 minutes, must have seemed
especially startling in the Concertgebouw's elevated surroundings. Even to
those familiar with Andriessen's Volharding style, the length and ambition
of the new piece lifted it onto a different plane. And the ensemble was not
just larger than De Volharding, but unusual by any standards, as the four
oboes of the work's opening immediately declared. Whether or not your
reaction was favourable, it was undeniable that 'there had been nothing like it
before!'[27]

In the Netherlands, the installation of *De Staat* as 'the standard-bearer for
contemporary Dutch music'[28] began early. 'How do you describe the sparks
[*sterreltjes*; literally, 'little stars'] caused by the blow of Louis Andriessen's *De
Staat*?' asked Elmer Schönberger at the beginning of his review of the
premiere. Schönberger dwelt on Andriessen's distinctive use of the techniques
of American minimalism, and suggested, pointedly, that Philip Glass related
to Andriessen as Carl Orff did to Stravinsky.[29] J. Reichenfeld, writing in the
NRC Handelsblad, found the music's 'rhetorical fury' an appropriate response
to the Plato, but also wielding an impact quite independently of the text.
Andriessen's brand of minimalist '*monotonie*' was, for Reichenfeld, 'vital' and

---

[27] Elmer Schönberger in conversation with the author, March 2002. Joël Bons,
artistic director of the Nieuw Ensemble, recalls the event in similar terms (private
conversation).

[28] Frits van der Waa, review of the premiere of the two-piano version of *De Staat*,
De Volkskrant, 17 November 1984, p. 11.

[29] Schönberger 1976.

'full of surprising elements'.[30] In *Trouw*, R. N. Degens found the piece 'exceptionally gripping', although he hazarded the opinion that the work was easier to appreciate if one forgot the 'extra-musical pretensions with which the music is saddled'.[31] Rutger Schoute in *Het Parool* was less enthusiastic. The trance-like state invoked by the repetitive processes of the 'modern American sound-mystics' prevented any real engagement with Plato's text, and the whole was cursed by the 'acoustic stupefaction' caused by amplification – a 'technique that makes all skill in orchestration superfluous'.[32]

Schoute's reservations notwithstanding, *De Staat* soon received further national and international acclaim, winning the 1977 UNESCO International Rostrum of Composers prize, and the prestigious Matthijs Vermeulen Prize in the same year. These prizes and the recording of the Amsterdam premiere resulted in unprecedented international exposure for Andriessen, and new institutional esteem in his home country. Within five years of giving up the itinerant, highly unglamorous lifestyle of the Orkest De Volharding, he was appointed the Holland Festival's first resident 'composer and commentator' in 1981, an event that climaxed with an 'Andriessen Night' in the Concert-gebouw. *De Staat*, which had been performed in Warsaw and Copenhagen as well as successfully revived at the Holland Festival in 1978, had laid the ground for this elevation to the status of foremost Dutch composer. At the time of the 1981 Festival, Andriessen expressed some ambivalence about this outcome:

> The success of *De Staat* had a peculiar effect on me. I had to realize how difficult it was to pin down what *I* thought was relevant … rather than doing the things I believed the world expected of me after *De Staat*. It took me three years to get to a point where I could once again do just what I fancied doing. (Andriessen, in De Beer 1981)[33]

It would be wrong, though, to give the impression that *De Staat* met with this level of success everywhere. The treatment meted out by British critics is a case in point. The first British performance, by an underprepared London Sinfonietta in January 1983,[34] did little to convert newcomers to Andriessen's

---

[30] J. Reichenfeld, 'Razende composities van Konrad Boehmer en Louis Andriessen', *NRC Handelsblad*, 29 November 1976, p. 6.

[31] R. N. Degens, 'Muziek en politiek met Boehmer en Andriessen', *Trouw*, 29 November 1976, p. 9.

[32] Rutger Schoute, '"Staat" verdooft', *Het Parool*, 29 November 1976, p. 7.

[33] See also Andriessen and Schönberger 1981, p. 11.

[34] Keith Potter, who knew the work from the Donemus recording, laid the problems

music. Dominic Gill, writing in the *Financial Times*, observed that the piece 'seems to last about two hours, actually lasts about half an hour, and drives you crazy after two minutes' and asserted that it 'has nothing whatever to do with Plato's Republic, beyond the reference in the title and the (incidental) inclusion of a Platonic text'.[35] Meirion Bowen thought the work 'exhausting to play and exhausting to listen to' and wondered whether its ethos was not 'every bit as authoritarian as Plato' – a criticism to which I shall return later in this chapter.[36] Felix Aprahamian, meanwhile, dismissed Andriessen's work as simply 'half an hour of fortissimo bowing and blowing in relentless motor rhythms'.[37] The critics' reservations echoed the reaction to Hoketus's visit to London a year earlier, which expressed suspicions about the group's 'populist stance' in which 'crude underlying principle is closely linked with simple rhetoric', and described the performance as 'numbing'.[38]

A common grievance, in the reviews of both the 1983 performance and a further British performance by the Sinfonietta in 1992, concerned the music's political subtext. Richard Morrison, writing in *The Times*, summed up the general feeling by referring to 'possibly the year's most pretentious programme-note', which 'somehow equated this brutal and frantic blast of post-minimalist noise with a statement about the artist's position in society'.[39] It is interesting that Andriessen's programme note should have been singled out for this accolade. One might have thought that, in its directness of language, avoidance of technical jargon and engagement with the most fundamental questions about the role of music in society, it would be viewed as a model of down-to-earth accessibility. The sticking point was presumably not the note *per se* but the very notion that music might seek to be overtly 'relevant', thus contravening the critics' cherished belief that serious contemporary music (as opposed to pop) should function on a purely aesthetic level. And it is an attitude that extended to the academic field in Britain – where one might have hoped that Andriessen's interest in cultural and

---

of the performance squarely at the door of insufficient rehearsal; see his review in *Classical Music*, 5 March 1983, p. 17.

[35] Dominic Gill, 'Textual triptych', *Financial Times*, 15 January 1983, p. 12.

[36] Meirion Bowen, review of London Sinfonietta concert, *The Guardian*, 15 January 1983, p. 6.

[37] Felix Aprahamian, 'A quartet of beauty', *Sunday Times*, 16 January 1983, p. 39.

[38] Stephen Walsh, 'Down to the bare minimal', *Observer*, 22 November 1981, and Paul Griffiths, review of Hoketus, *The Times*, 17 November 1981, p. 8.

[39] Richard Morrison, 'Brought to life at last', *The Times*, 26 June 1992. The title refers to the first performance in the same concert of a neglected Copland score.

philosophical ideas would carry greater weight. Reviewing the second recording of *De Staat*, Arnold Whittall admitted to a preference for the 'maximalism' of Carter or Maxwell Davies over the 'immediate but easily exhaustible impact' of *De Staat*'s 'minimalism'.[40] This interpretative outlook presumably accounts for the single, rather slight paragraph that Andriessen received in Whittall's weighty survey of *Musical Composition in the Twentieth Century*.[41] More grudging still is the single sentence accorded to Andriessen in Paul Griffiths's *Modern Music and After* from 1995 – extraordinary, given the extent of his popularity and influence in Britain and America by this time.[42]

The story of *De Staat*'s reception in Britain points to an underestimation by British critics of the extent to which this piece – and, to a certain extent, Andriessen's music more generally – is the outcome of a comprehensive reassessment of the very criteria by which contemporary music should be judged. In particular, negative assessments of the work typically overlook the intimate relation between the piece and the performance context on which it depends, and is partly 'about'. *De Staat* is grounded in assumptions about performers, performance style, venues and audiences, none of which have necessarily been readily reproducible outside the Netherlands, or even Amsterdam. It is demonstrably *not* just another configuration of notes and rhythms, to be assessed alongside all the other modern scores against which critics customarily exercise their aesthetic sensibilities. It is in its attitude to performance, rather than its formal devices or individual fusion of influences, that *De Staat* arguably comes closest to 'the alteration of the state' about which Plato was so nervous.

The fact that *De Staat* has at least one foot in the world of 'official music' – which is to say, that it is played (as it was from the beginning) in traditional concert venues by established ensembles of classical musicians, and subsequently found itself recorded and promoted by a giant American multi-national company – tends to disguise the extent to which the work is a continuation of the distinctive, 'counter-cultural' performing practice of the Orkest De Volharding. As Andriessen relates in Chapter 5, *De Staat* was never intended for the musicians of De Volharding, but it was nevertheless an 'extension of De Volharding'. On another occasion, he described *De Staat* as

---

    [40] Arnold Whittall, review of LP of *De Staat*, *Gramophone*, July 1994, p. 138.

    [41] Arnold Whittall, *Musical Composition in the Twentieth Century* (Oxford: Oxford University Press, 1999), p. 344. Whittall has made substantial amends since then: see Whittall 2001 and 2003.

    [42] Paul Griffiths, *Modern Music and After: Directions since 1945* (Oxford: Clarendon Press, 1995), p. 275.

'actually a piece for De Volharding, but with more musicians and a conductor. Everything that De Volharding couldn't do ended up in *De Staat*' (Andriessen 1996b, p. 118). It is significant in this respect that, as I have noted elsewhere, the conception and composition of *De Staat* spanned precisely the period of Andriessen's involvement with De Volharding. The style of performance that he favours for *De Staat* – closer to Count Basie and Stan Kenton than Bruckner and Mahler – is the most obvious way in which it reflects this connection. However, as he makes clear, *De Staat* goes beyond De Volharding too. This was not simply a matter of having more and different instruments at his disposal, but also of technical difficulty: the musicians of De Volharding 'had certain limitations in terms of their performance abilities' (Andriessen, in Trochimczyk (ed.) 2002, p. 135) and *De Staat* undoubtedly provided a welcome release. Some of the anger of the piece can be read as the product of the realization that the 'ideal' working practices of De Volharding – its critique of official musical performance – brought with them severe constraints for more purely musical expressions of anger towards society. It seems you could have one, but not both:

> I believe that the fury in *De Staat*, BANG BANG BANG the whole time, is even more personal than *The Last Day* (1997).... I had a lot to rage about. I wanted to do things, amongst others with De Volharding, and I must say that some things were successful.... But I wanted to keep on shouting and De Volharding couldn't play my shouting any more. I needed more trumpets, faster rhythms and time changes. And then that – *De Staat* – came out of it. (Andriessen 2002, pp. 146–47)

In returning in *De Staat* to a large ensemble, classical musicians and a conductor, Andriessen necessarily embraced elements of orchestral practice. And yet, as we saw at the end of Chapter 1, he remained vocally critical at this time of the dominance of orchestras in musical life. Indeed, he has kept at a distance from the 'fussy, bourgeois world'[43] of the symphony orchestra ever since, with the exception of *De Snelheid* (1984), which aroused great hostility amongst the San Francisco Symphony Orchestra and confirmed all his worst fears about orchestral musicians (Trochimczyk (ed.) 2002, p. 153). Accordingly, it was important for him to be able to account for *De Staat*'s cautious rapprochement with orchestral tradition as something other than a regressive move. This he was to do with the claim that the piece, rather than rejecting orchestral practice outright, existed in a 'polemical relation with the

---

[43] Andriessen, in Op de Coul 1979. This lengthy interview is one of Andriessen's most extended statements on the failings of the symphony orchestra.

symphony orchestra' (Andriessen 1990b, p. 148). In other words, in characteristically Brechtian fashion the object of criticism, instead of being ignored, is incorporated as part of a dialectical arrangement in order to comment more effectively upon it. Small, alternative performing ensembles such as De Volharding were unable to do this, which meant that the challenge of the orchestral tradition passed without direct comment (ibid., pp. 148–49).

This polemical relation exists at a number of levels. First, there is the question of dimension and ambition. *De Staat* adopts some of the values of the symphonic repertoire in this regard. The piece is extended in length, comprises 'abstract' musical material (that is, it is predominantly instrumental), and is intended for concentrated listening. On the other hand, it completely shuns the finesse and refinement that tend to accompany these characteristics in the established orchestral repertoire. As we saw in Chapter 3, the work's form is abrupt and its musical materials generally rude and unembellished: what you hear is what you get. This crudity of content, far from signalling a failing of creativity or imagination, is a central premise, for it is Andriessen's way of trying to wrest the large-scale musical statement from the clutches of bourgeois connoisseurship. *De Staat* proposes, in other words, that extended musical forms may remain valid and even urgent as social statements, but only as long as they are stripped entirely free of the decorative, 'culinary' elements whose principal function is to gratify the taste and cultivation of the bourgeois music-lover. (In this respect, other avant-garde music – Andriessen cites in particular music from Paris – is barely distinguishable from 'a confectioner's in Beethovenstraat'; see Koning and Jansen 1981, p. 13.[44]) Andriessen's later music, in becoming more structurally intricate, lowers its guard on this front: works like *De Tijd* and *De Snelheid*, their uncompromising idiom notwithstanding, invite knowledgeable appreciation and in so doing sit more easily in the concert hall. *De Staat*, uniquely, seeks to combine a renewed confidence in the value of purely musical discourse – for it is Andriessen's most ambitious concert work since 1970 – with a continuing refusal of the trappings and motivations of the 'ruling classes' who have historically been autonomous music's principal cultivators and consumers. This may be an impossible task – the inseparability of artistic appreciation and the privileged lifestyles of the dominant classes has been persuasively argued by Pierre Bourdieu, amongst others (see Fowler 1997) – but it is an ideal on which *De Staat* firmly sets its sights.

The ensemble for which *De Staat* is scored represents a second level at

---

[44] Beethovenstraat is a boutique-lined boulevard in Amsterdam, just south of the Concertgebouw.

which it engages polemically with the orchestra. By comparison with De Volharding, the 31 musicians required for *De Staat*, and the incorporation of strings and woodwind, certainly make the work's scoring seem 'orchestral'. On the other hand, violins – the principal spokespeople of the symphony orchestra – are completely absent. And quite apart from the general unusualness of the ensemble, the presence of electric guitars and amplification contravenes two taboos of orchestral performance: that regarding instruments associated with pop music, and that regarding the 'purity' of unamplified acoustic sound. The utterly distinctive *sonority* of *De Staat*'s ensemble – punchy and steely at full pelt, reedily sinewy elsewhere – in itself passes comment on the symphony orchestra, commandeering its power and potential for timbral contrast, while rejecting its genteel cushioning and homogenizing blend.

Guitars, keyboards, amplification and no or reduced strings have since become staple ingredients of Andriessen's 'great revolutionary orchestra of the twenty-first century' (Andriessen 1990a, p. 100), various forms of which have been the basis for the series of large works, beginning with *De Staat*, of the last 25 years. The grandiose tendencies of Andriessen's scoring reached their peak with *De Laatste Dag* (1996), the original version of which was written for the combined Asko, Schönberg, Netherlands Wind, and Nieuw Ensembles. The financial and institutional support on which such scoring is dependent arguably risks precisely the kind of imbalance of resources of which Andriessen was so critical in the early seventies; it is certainly a world away from the flexibility and portability that was such a prized aspect of De Volharding and other small ensembles of that era. On the other hand, the appeal for Andriessen of his twenty-first-century orchestra is not simply a matter of Wagnerian self-indulgence. Much of his mature music – and certainly *De Staat* – celebrates, in quite specific ways, the communal qualities of making music in a large group: it is as if he wants to prove that such mass performance need not imply alienation and submission, but can on the contrary be a symbol of solidarity and collectivity.[45] The full weight and power of Andriessen's ensemble is periodically exploited to this end in *De Staat*: one thinks of the four unison notes that abruptly shatter the preceding minimalist haze at bar 492, or the endlessly repeated five-note figure at bar 567 which (eventually) involves the whole ensemble.

However, it is a particular kind of collectivity that is especially characteristic: namely, a hard-won, industrious group effort. *De Staat* is not simply a

---

[45] This aspect of the piece is naturally lost in the two-piano version recorded by Cees van Zeeland and Gerard Bouwhuis (Attacca Babel 8949–2).

celebration of many people playing together, but specifically a celebration of many people achieving something *difficult*. The sheer stamina required of the performers, most of whom are playing most of the time at high volume and high speed, is a manifestation of this. (Andriessen's interest in the 'staying power' of individual musicians (Andriessen 1972, p. 131) can of course be traced back to the Orkest De Volharding.) And certain passages seem to have the laying down of a performative challenge as their principal *raison d'être*. The unison semiquaver melodies are a case in point – a demonstration of sustained exertion on the part of the performers, as much as a 'purely musical' statement. Likewise, in the extended section of antiphonal hocketing from bar 791, the performers' strenuous attempts to prevent the interlocking parts slipping out of sync provides much of the music's excitement. Throughout the score, performance markings vividly exhort the full and complete involvement of the performers, making apparently straightforward passages more demanding than they might otherwise be. Thus the two pianos are requested to play several single-line passages 'with two hands'; and in the final canon every note is not only treble *forte* but accented and staccato. Willem Jan Otten has spoken of the 'sense of identification' a listener feels with individual performers in Andriessen's music, the 'fervent hope' that a musician will 'keep on playing the notes exactly on time, for the composition is made in such a way that doing so has become "a matter of life and death"' (Otten 1994, p. 15). From this point of view Meirion Bowen's slighting remark that the piece is 'exhausting to play and exhausting to listen to' accurately identifies an important aspect of Andriessen's philosophy of performance.

The extreme difficulty of the music requires musicians who are highly trained – and this represents a third level at which *De Staat* engages with orchestral tradition. For all that Andriessen requires the performers of *De Staat* to leave behind their classical training when it comes to articulation and tone quality, the music demands that they be excellent readers, and have a strong technical mastery of their instrument. As we have seen, *De Staat* is full of precisely what the Orkest De Volharding, with its improvisatory approximations and laissez-faire attitudes, could not do; it makes a point of showcasing the performers' technical skill and discipline. *De Staat* is not the first of Andriessen's pieces to treat musical performers as industrious labourers. *Workers Union* forms an obvious precedent. Less obviously, the unifying idea of the *Symphonies of the Netherlands* is, according to the composer, 'hard work, the same kind of hard work as dragging a plough through the flat Dutch polder fields. Heavy work and always the same.'[46]

---

[46] Composer's preface to the score of *Symphonies of the Netherlands*.

Another point brought up by Meirion Bowen here raises its head – the question of authoritarianism. Does Andriessen not reinscribe the conditions that he worked so hard to eliminate – in other words, the submission of the performer to the controlling will of the composer? Paul Griffiths's reaction to *Hoketus*, that it was 'a sad experience to see a dozen people tying themselves to so brutish a treadmill', implicitly levels this very charge.[47]

One way to answer this is to point to the degree to which Andriessen's music, far from subordinating the performing musicians, is in fact principally *about* them. A work like *Hoketus* hardly exploits performers in the service of some elaborate personal conception on the part of the composer. Rather, the work exists precisely in order to allow the musicians to display their virtuosity and perseverance; its exceedingly formulaic processes make sense only when viewed in these terms. The same concern – that the music should be as much about the performers as the composer – applies to a lesser but still significant degree for *De Staat*. (Nor is this a piece likely to be favoured by conductors wishing to enhance their personal glory: the rhythmic unanimity of a good performance hangs more on the mutual awareness of the players than on melodramatics from the podium.) Andriessen, indeed, far from neglecting performers, has spoken of them as his first and even primary audience: 'most music I write is written, I think, first of all for the performers' (Andriessen 1978, p. 51). The idea that composers should be mindful of the preferences of the performers was of course intrinsic to De Volharding's founding philosophy.

This amounts to more than empty idealism, however, only in a musical culture in which performers have real control over what they play. *De Staat* was predicated on the existence of ensembles able to determine their repertoire democratically. It was Andriessen's explicit intention that only musicians who *wanted* to undertake the challenges of the piece should find themselves playing it: as he made clear, 'I hope I'll never write another work that musicians in paid employment will be forced to play against their will' (Andriessen 1977b, p. 44). Crucially, the developing ensemble culture in the Netherlands, behind which Andriessen had been one of the principal driving forces, meant that this was far from being an untenable position. The Netherlands Wind Ensemble, for whom the work was written and who gave

---

[47] Griffiths, review of Hoketus, *The Times*, 17 November 1981, p. 8. Kevin Whitehead describes *De Volharding* in similar terms: '*Volharding*'s relentless tuttis, with no opportunities to lay out and catch one's breath, are a little like denying your workers a coffee break, making them sit at the stamping machine ten hours a day' (Whitehead 1999, p. 243).

the first performances, operated in precisely such a democratic fashion. It comprised a core of musicians each of whom, in addition to participating as performers, had artistic responsibility for individual concerts. Freelance musicians were then hired on the basis of their predisposition towards different programmes: in the case of *De Staat*, the musicians approached mostly differed from those used for the Ensemble's concerts of classical repertoire.[48] That there were plenty of musicians ready and willing to throw themselves into the challenges of *De Staat* from the earliest years of its existence is amply demonstrated by the blistering live recording accompanying this book.

As we have seen, however, the question of oppressiveness does not apply exclusively to reluctant performers; it is also evidently a feature of many listeners' experiences of *De Staat*. In 1983 and 1992 the majority of British critics clearly had their patience stretched to and beyond breaking point, and even the otherwise sympathetic reviewer of the 1978 revival in *Mens en Melodie* admitted that, 'for sensitive souls, the enormous number of decibels that this piece ... unceasingly casts forth [*verspreidt*] is certainly oppressive'.[49] It is not just the perpetual loudness of the piece – sometimes exacerbated in live performance by levels of amplification that go well beyond the composer's request for good balance[50] – that causes this reaction. *De Staat* also stretches its material to unlikely, even intolerable lengths; the seemingly interminable march following the central choral section is only the most obvious of many passages in this respect. The work is not without its *longueurs*. And its abrupt formal non sequiturs further test a listener's willingness to stay the course.

There are a number of possible explanations for these features of the score. For a start, Andriessen's durational scheme exerts certain demands which sometimes mean ignoring the 'natural' tendencies of the material that fills it. This stance – the adherence to pre-compositional design regardless of alternative options that might be suggested by the music itself, or by considerations of listener psychology – is in line with serial orthodoxy, which

---

[48] I am indebted to Geert van Keulen for these details regarding the Netherlands Wind Ensemble. Van Keulen, as well as being bass clarinettist with the Ensemble, had artistic responsibility for the concerts that included the first performances of *De Staat*.

[49] 'Concerten in het Holland Festival 1978' [editorial review], *Mens en Melodie*, **33** (August 1978), 250.

[50] The instruction in the score is that 'all instruments are dynamically balanced by electrical amplification'. Andriessen's priorities are perfectly clear – 'I do not use amplification in order to make the sound louder but in order to achieve a refined balance by amplifying parts of the ensemble' (Andriessen 1997/1999a, p. 299) – but are sometimes ignored by sound technicians.

of course played a significant part in Andriessen's early formation as a composer. One should also recall, however, the importance in Andriessen's early years of a different avant-garde tradition: that associated with John Cage and other New York 'experimentalists'. The treatment of time by composers like Cage and Earle Brown has remained a preoccupation of Andriessen's ever since his initial infatuation with their music in the late fifties and early sixties. In 1981 he commented,

> What attracted me to Cage was his very exciting way of dealing with time.... For me it had the effect that you had to go as far as you can; that you must immerse yourself deeply in things such as duration.... *Melodie* is unthinkable without Cage; I can also point to places in *De Staat* or *Mausoleum* that are concerned with the 'unhistorical time-consciousness', if you will, that arose at this time. (In Bernlef 1981, pp. 89, 94).

Andriessen again mentions Cage as an influence on *De Staat* in the interview contained in this book (Ch. 5). In some ways, though, a more apt comparison is with Stockhausen, whose music in the sixties and early seventies evinced a similar interest in new concepts of time, while also remaining perceptibly connected to European musical traditions. Stockhausen's *Trans* (1971) and *Inori* (1974) – pieces that Andriessen openly admires (see Ford 1993, p. 84) – are gesturally bold and adopt recognizable forms of pitch and rhythmic organization. Yet in their ritualistic obsessiveness and staticity, they completely abandon conventional expectations regarding formal contrast and development. Much the same can be said of parts of *De Staat* – and nowhere more so than immediately after the central choral section, where the entire ensemble pounds out a rebarbative rising and falling figure for three and a half long minutes.[51] Andriessen associates this passage with a visual image that arose early in the composition of *De Staat*, of a huge wall slowly falling over the listener (Trochimczyk (ed.) 2002, p. 103): in this case at least, the oppressiveness of lengthily protracted material is intrinsic to his conception. Critics' frustration at the long-windedness of parts of *De Staat* tends to overlook the continuing importance to Andriessen of this experimental tradition of reconceiving time – a tradition that inherently flies in the face of conventional notions of 'good' musical form.

---

[51] This is the only place in the work where there is a substantial difference between the two editions of the score. In the original Donemus score, the dynamic 'waves' recede to *piano* or *pianissimo*, whereas in the 1994 Boosey and Hawkes score the quietest dynamic is *forte*. Reinbert de Leeuw's 1990 recording adheres to the revised dynamics.

A second, possibly more important explanation for these 'difficult' aspects of *De Staat* is Andriessen's interest, already alluded to in this chapter, in repudiating bourgeois standards of taste. When Antony Bye complains (in a review in the *Musical Times*) that the piece is 'too long for its undistinguished material, relentless and manipulative in its agitprop insistence and crude in its juxtapositions',[52] he is effectively pointing to various ways in which the work is a *success*. *De Staat* lacks 'good taste' in its unrelenting volume and general lack of musical decorum – and that is its intention. The idea that political progressiveness goes hand in hand with a nose-thumbing attitude towards notions of artistic refinement had been a defining part of the Orkest De Volharding's ideology of performance, as we saw in Chapter 2. In his article on *De Maatregel*, Andriessen highlighted the accusation of the music critic Heinrich Strobel that Eisler's original music was 'naive and too simple' as an indication that it was doing its job properly: its aim was the 'political education' of the workers for whom it was written, not the 'musical pleasure of Strobel Esq.' (Andriessen 1975, pp. 429–30). *De Staat* risks being similarly misunderstood if the generally accepted criteria for assessing concert music are applied.

Of course, this is not to say that *De Staat* was intended as a tool for the oppressed. In 1978 Andriessen realistically estimated his audience to comprise 'the progressive middle classes ... aged between 25 and 40' (in Op de Coul 1979). Leaving the Orkest De Volharding necessarily also meant leaving behind aspirations to reach the broadest range of listeners. The fact that *De Staat* principally addresses the middle classes is consistent, nevertheless, with its 'polemical relation' to the orchestra. As we have already noted, *De Staat* complies with some of the expectations of the traditional classical concert audience: its length and the predominance of purely instrumental music give it a certain conventional, 'artistic' character. (That the work is susceptible to a measure of purely 'aesthetic' appreciation is fully demonstrated by my own discussion in Chapter 3.) But at the same time its unapologetic coarseness of expression withdraws the possibility of the sort of comfortable, self-congratulatory reverence often associated with the classical concert audience. And this is not the only respect in which *De Staat* makes an intervention with regard to the conventional role of concert-goers. The relationship between audience and performers is also altered. Where the symphony orchestra comprises an army of labourers, dressed in servile uniform and toiling for the pleasure of the paying audience, *De Staat* dramatically levels the ground, making the listeners' task as arduous as the performers'. The work's sustained

---

[52] Antony Bye, 'Dutch courage', *Musical Times* (March 1993), 139.

volume and repetitive insistence present a formidable test of endurance to any listener's powers of concentration – and in their doing so, the hierarchical arrangement separating performers and audience is at least partially removed.

In an interview about *De Staat*, Andriessen once said, 'I think of writing a kind of musical criticism which is interesting for people who are critical themselves – that's the best way to put it' (Andriessen 1990b, p. 155). *De Staat*'s comprehensive reassessment of the ground rules of concert performance presents an implicit critique of conventional orchestral practice. And in so doing, it joins other layers of critique identified earlier in this chapter: critique of the sentiments of Plato, and (in a characteristically dialectical fashion) of the premises of American minimalism. It would be completely wrong, however, to give the impression that the piece has a predominantly negative cast. With its formidable energy, gestural flamboyance, and improvisatory swagger, it could hardly be further from the sort of bleak musical visions sometimes associated with critical philosophies.[53] It is the particular achievement of *De Staat* that harsh polemic and hedonistic pleasure are treated as necessary partners, not irreconcilable opposites. Instead of being kept hostilely at bay, listeners are embraced by the music's immediacy and communicativeness, and thus invited to participate in the critical stance. Andriessen's response to Plato's restrictive vision of the ideal state takes the form, then, of the creation of an alternative musical 'community', one that extends beyond his musicians to include the audience and – by encouraging changed perceptions amongst them – the wider world of which they are a part.

---

[53] For instance, a number of German avant-garde composers in the early seventies, driven in part by the critical theory of the Frankfurt School, expressed their rejection of 'society' through a parallel rejection of conventional categories of musical sound. See Elke Hockings, 'Helmut Lachenmann's concept of rejection', *Tempo*, **193** (July 1995), 4–14.

Chapter 5

An Interview with Louis Andriessen

[LA:] For me *De Staat* is a kind of extension of De Volharding.[1]

[RA:] *Right ... well, that's where I wanted to start. I'm interested that at the end of the score of* De Staat *you wrote '1972–1976'. But in your conversations with Maja Trochimczyk you say that the piece is highly improvisatory in its construction ...*

Yeah, but that doesn't have too much to do with the dates. I didn't work for four years constantly on that piece, because at the same time I worked with De Volharding and did other things. It took a lot of reflection, you might say, in order for the piece to reach its final state. So the first sketches came from 1972, and the piece was finally finished in 1976. But it's not true to say that it took me four years to write it; in actual fact it was more like two years, maximum. But I learnt to *reflect* for the first time with this piece. I could get rid of a lot of things connected to De Volharding – discussions about aesthetics, politics and so on. I was performing a lot, which I liked, but it also meant that I had the space and possibility to reflect upon such a large piece. Particularly about what I could not do with De Volharding – things to do with technical possibilities, and singing.

I hear different parts of the piece as having resonances with some of your other works in that period. There are moments that sound a bit like De Volharding, *and moments that sound a bit like* Il Principe *or the* Symphonies of the Netherlands. *Would these resonances reflect the period at which parts of the piece were being written?*

Yeah, I'd say so .... The wind orchestra piece [*Symphonies of the Netherlands*] is what I called, at that time, '*De Staat* explained for working-class people'! That's a quotation actually. In Holland there's a quite famous writer called Gerard Reve – he's one of these Decadent, Romantic writers.[2] It's very local.

---

[1] This conversation with Louis Andriessen was held at the end of September 2002 in his Amsterdam apartment overlooking the Keizersgracht.

[2] Andriessen requested the capital letters here.

I don't like it very much. Anyway, at that time, one of his articles was on the graphic artist Pannekoek, and he called it 'The etchings of Pannekoek explained for working-class people'.[3]

Did you always intend De Staat *to be for an ensemble other than De Volharding?*

Yes. I think even when I started writing it, the first idea was probably for the oboes – maybe it wasn't the first idea, but oboes were very important – and we had no oboes in De Volharding. Oboe playing is an important culture in Holland, and always has been. It's a different style of playing from the French and from the Germans. That was my symbol for Greek music. At that time, the Netherlands Wind Ensemble was very active. They had a pre-history in the fifties – especially for Mozart and so on. And then there was a new generation of players, people of my age, who wanted to combine all the Mozart stuff with new music. They worked basically as a group of wind instruments, sometimes with brass, and then, because composers wanted to write new pieces for them, they added other instruments to it. So it became really one of the 'new ensembles' in fact, and they did a lot of new stuff. The 'Political-Demonstrative Experimental concert', which happened in 1968, was already a project of the Netherlands Wind Ensemble.

Can I ask you about the sketches to De Staat? *They don't include very much in terms of the small detail of the piece.*

Certainly there are notes for the tetrachords – but I didn't keep the pre-sketches. In a very few cases I think it's relevant to keep them, but 80 per cent I throw away. You cannot keep everything – too much chaos! The sketch you have there was written very late, let's say the last half a year. Before that, I composed a lot in piano score, which I do all the time. For all the larger works I have almost complete and very clean piano scores. For *De Tijd* they are written on five staves, six sometimes if you count the singing – so not really playable on the piano. But it gives me an overview of longer periods, to allow me to play through and get a sense of the larger spans. I did that also for *De Staat*, but at a certain stage I started to make a sketch for the score. This I don't do any more, because I'm now spoilt: I have a very clean piano score and then I ask my computer genius Chris Abelen to make open, empty pages for the score, and then I just fill them in. The piano score is down at the bottom of the

---

[3] Gerard Kornelis van het Reve, *Veertien Etsen van Frans Lodewijk Pannekoek voor Arbeiders verklaard* ('Fourteen etchings by Frans Lodewijk Pannekoek explained for workers') (Amsterdam: Thomas Rap, 1967).

page and then, with the mouse – I give him indications of what is going where – he just moves it. Amazing! It makes my life easy.

So a lot of things are not there? You probably know more about the sketches than I do, because I don't sentimentally look through them. But I do remember making notes about the tetrachords. I find it much more interesting now, looking back at it, than I did at that time, this idea of considering *all* four-note chords as tetrachords. That means that the intervals are often larger than major or minor seconds of course. It's like the opening chord of the Stockhausen piano piece, which I consider a tetrachord too.[4] From that point on, when the intervals are larger than the seconds, then the tetrachord can be the basis for both harmony and melody. I see it as one thing – the Stockhausen chord, and the simple 'do-re-mi-fa', as the same material – very unscientifical! But that's part of art of course.

So the tetrachords were something you reflected upon a lot.

Yes. The whole idea started with the Plato, which I had read a long time before … I've forgotten when. One of the things you learnt at the Conservatory was: Greek music? – that means tetrachords! And being a contemporary composer, that means much more than 'do-re-mi-fa'. I think that was a very stimulating idea with which to start writing the piece.

There are some tetrachords that come back regularly, and others that seem much more intuitive and occasional. Is that a correct understanding of how the tetrachords are working in the piece?

Looking back at it, it is very evident that there is a preference for certain tetrachords. Certainly these include ones that are not used in Western tonal music, and some that are typically Indonesian. There are some simple ones in fact also, like the central choir – 'do-re-mi-fa', with the added A natural but basically a very simple tetrachord. But I do avoid the normal ones, let us say. Stravinsky doesn't. Stravinsky has in the *Sacre* basically very simple tetrachords all the time. I was specifically interested in the wider, more chromatic ones.

Now, systematically, I didn't decide to use some and not others – there was not a system at all. But certainly a musical preference as to which ones to use and which ones not. And I do avoid a lot of the tonal things. It was the whole idea to be provocative and aggressive and not nice and sweet! And I think all the modal tetrachords would be too sweet and too nice.

---

[4] Andriessen is referring to Stockhausen's Klavierstück IX (1961), which opens with a four-note chord repeated 139 times.

I wanted to ask you about modes. In your note to the piece you say it has 'nothing to do with Greek music', except for the oboes and tetrachords. But in the sketches you have this chart of the Greek modes, which comes from the note by Arnold van Akkeren which appears with the original LP recording ...

Yes, with the emotional descriptions. They came from what Arnold told me. But what's really interesting, and which I didn't learn about from school, was that they defined the modes upside down – from top to bottom. I learnt that from Arnold.

And the names are different from the medieval church modes ...

Yes, they're all mixed up. Arnold van Akkeren was my man ... he was my guru, and I just followed what he thought at that time was the most probable way of approaching the subject.

There's still a fair bit of confusion about it. But I've had difficulty finding any clear connection between this chart and the piece.

Well, it's basically only studying, like you study counterpoint before you become a composer.

But you could imagine a setting of the Plato that's quite pictorial. So when Plato's talking about a certain mode having a military character or a decadent character, you could imagine a setting that's very illustrative and that uses those modes in that way. But that appears to be completely contrary to what you wanted to do.

Yes – it doesn't function at all like that. After two thousand years we have somewhat more developed ideas about music! This chart is similar to what I have done for other pieces: do some studying, on the theoretical and historical background, just to get the mind going, then start composing. You may try to find parallels – whether bits of the music are Phrygian or Dorian – but I doubt if it will make very much sense. I think the influences, coming from Cage and other American composers, and of Far Eastern music, is certainly more important – this is much more evident. This [points to chart of modes] is much too close to plainchant, to our own culture. It never sounds exotic. For me the Greek thing was exotic.

So the Indonesian scales were an analogy ...

Yeah, more Greek than the Greek! I should tell you a story about Ravel, it's not very well known. It comes from the biography by Roland-Manuel, who was a good friend in his last years. Ravel was already not in good health – he had dementia praecox. His friends took him to Morocco in '32 or so. They were standing on this square in Marrakesh, and there were two musicians playing on a flute and some drums – very simple things. When Ravel got back to the hotel he said, 'I can write something which sounds much more Arab than that'! It is true of course.

Let's talk about harmony. I think Elmer Schönberger wrote about the importance of the idea of 'the chord as an object' to your music – that a chord has its own autonomy and that it doesn't need to participate in a syntax or voice-leading.[5] There's lots in De Staat *that reflects that. But there are also passages where the harmony is moving more swiftly, where I hear an underlying tonality, or conventional tonal syntax …*

At that time I did not really think about voice-leading. Since then I've completely changed and now find it extremely important. In *De Staat* I do take a chord and transpose it. But at that time harmonic progression wasn't as interesting as the montage approach – it should be shocking and surprising and sudden. Being a child from a family of musicians I have very good ears, so there may be good reasons for why which chord came after which. But still, at that time I found it interesting to use a limited amount of musical material, to use transposition where necessary, and not think too much about what I would now consider to be *allusions* to tonal functions.

I want to show you the sections I'm thinking about …

It starts to be evident in the places where there are good bass notes, no? You identify this place [b. 552 onwards] because there are moving bass notes … A–D–A, which supports the harmony.

There's a passage earlier too. I hear this passage [b. 518 onwards] in tonal terms, essentially, with lots of chromatic complication. It seems to be to do with movement by thirds: C–E–A♭.

That's not impossible. I'm too far away from it – you can have a different interpretation. This harmony here [points to b. 519] is based upon a four-part chord [at the piano]:

---

5 See Schönberger 1996, p. 213.

which you find in French Romantic music, and I know from my father that, especially in Chausson, you can add the C♯ to get this:

That is a French thing …

But also the movement by thirds is characteristic of Germanic late-Romantic music …

… but actually there are more notes in fact:

I do avoid octaves in the modes. And many of them go over an octave …

The minor ninth seems important …

Yeah. You can see this as a combination of two tetrachords in fact:

But I still see this as the Chausson chord. The C♯ would be the first to join it, then the E:

But I don't think there are any parallel major thirds – I'm no great fan of German late Romanticism …

I know, but I wondered if it might have come down through the French adoption of certain Wagnerian harmonic techniques ...

You're completely right. For example Chausson and *Parsifal*. And what I played just now is very close to the amazing Amfortas sequence in *Parsifal*. Chausson, and Duparc also, are very profoundly, and in an interesting way, influenced by Wagner.

And Debussy also.

He's different. More modal. They were very good friends of course. You know that Chausson died because he was on his bicycle on his way to the station to pick up Debussy. He fell off his bicycle and caught an infection.

You didn't ask me about the larger structure. The planning of the three choral sections was very carefully worked out. Before I started the piece, I had in mind what I call three 'caryatids' – three pillars that support the whole piece.

It's like a fixed frame within which you placed more spontaneous material ...

But on a very simple basis, because the central choral section starts right in the middle of the piece, and ends at the golden section. Then the wall falls down on you![6] This sextuplets section [bb. 725–90] was cut by John Adams when he did it in San Francisco.

Really?

Well, it's OK – more like a joke. He had a full house. He loved the piece, and he said 'I'm going to do that', but he took out the sextuplets so as not to worry the audience too much. He had thousands of people there. You know why – because he asked Keith Jarrett to play the Stravinsky Piano Concerto, which was a very good move. So you had all these people there. It was a fantastic success.

Still, it would be a very different piece without that section.

Yeah. '*De Staat* explained for yuppies', you might say!

Can I ask you about the metre in the central choral section? It's much more irregular than most of the rest of the piece.

Well, here it's very clear that the reason the bars are the way they are is because of the accents in the Greek. Sometimes I go against it, but in general

---

6 See Chapter 4, p. 129.

I wanted to stay close to the rhetorical sound of the speaking. When you read the text out loud, you'll get an idea of the rhythmical way in which it could have been spoken. Of course, when people speak they're using changing metre all the time. And it also has to do with the message in the text, and that's why the other two are different. Also for musical reasons. The last one's like a final chorale: it should be very … 'with pressure', very steady, like an old pastor. So I didn't use the speaking rhythms.

You've talked about De Staat *existing in a polemical relation with the symphony orchestra. What do you mean by that?*

Well, in the first case of course, the choice of the instruments. That is very clear. But at that time I meant it also in a more profound, philosophical way of thinking about musical communication. What I found important in *De Staat* is that there is not a hierarchy in the parts. That means that everybody is democratically justified in doing what he does. You don't have parts that are more interesting or less interesting, or more important or less important.

When I was watching the rehearsal last week, it really struck me how, in the fast unison melodies, the conductor wasn't really important. The music was saying to the musicians: you have to listen to each other. So for those periods it was much more like De Volharding, where there was no conductor and the musicians were working as an ensemble.

Yes, and that's related to the anti-symphony orchestra idea. As a musician, you have to be on the edge of your seat all the time. It's very difficult music. Now, in fact, it doesn't sound so difficult, but I want it to sound difficult – that's much better than when it's a slick performance.

That's like The Rite of Spring …

Same problem.

And yet although there's an element of rejecting the symphony orchestra, it's not a complete rejection. It's a large ensemble, it's an extended piece, quite grandiose. You said somewhere that you wanted to turn the weaponry of the symphony orchestra against itself … [7]

Yes, that's true. For important subjects you need the large ensembles. *De Tijd* doesn't work with two flutes and two clarinets. But the most important thing is that, even with *De Staat*, which is almost unplayable without classically

---

[7] Andriessen uses this expression in an interview with Kasper Jansen: '"De Staat" na kwart eeuw nog steeds actueel', *NRC Handelsblad*, 10 September 2001, p. 8.

trained symphony orchestra musicians, on the whole it is not played by symphony orchestras. So I am not confronted any more with musicians who don't like to play my music.

You've said that you're quite pleased that the music is difficult because it means it doesn't get performed between Brahms and Mozart ...[8]

But the difficulty is not technical – these guys can play anything. It's a musical difficulty, a psychological difficulty. The music doesn't belong in the symphony orchestra. It has too much to do with Count Basie, as I always say.

You've also talked about the difficulty of getting orchestral musicians to articulate in the way you like – more of a jazz-style articulation.

Yes – very important.

At the rehearsal, Reinbert de Leeuw was trying to get the horn players to produce the note immediately, rather than have a softer, more gradual attack. What's the appeal of that kind of articulation for you?

Reinbert once said, 'it should sound like a piano' – always a very sharp attack. But on the other hand, the attack should not be what I would call 'posh'. I think that classical music is highly over-articulated. I once heard on the radio an extremely mediocre little piece, a trio I think – it could have been any composer, totally uninteresting. But because it was so amazingly beautifully played – for *nothing* – it had to be a famous composer. I forget who it was, Mozart or Schubert probably. But the playing was much too beautiful for this extremely simple music. Schubert would have been totally surprised at this performance. So perfumed and refined – *tasteless* in fact, that's the funny thing. The kind of articulation I prefer is very much contrary to the classical, conservatoire training. I have had to fight that continually.

Jazz articulation gives you access to the person behind the instrument, where classical training seems to present an obstacle to that.

Yes. The metaphor is that when you write a B♭ for a symphony orchestra you get a B♭; when you write a B♭ for De Volharding you get De Volharding! Hoketus is another example. The music I write for smaller ensembles is really directly connected with the people who play it. *La Passione* is a very good example.[9] It's written around these two young musicians. Cristina [Zavalloni]

---

   [8] See Andriessen, in Koning and Jansen 1981, p. 13.
   [9] *La Passione* for voice, violin and ensemble (2002) received its first performance a week after this interview.

is a jazz singer. And I worked with Monica [Germino] for a long time on the problem of legato playing on the violin.

Singing is my main concern for the next twenty years – to change it. We have now changed instrumental playing quite a lot in Holland: the 'low-brow' instruments can play highly complex music very well, and the 'high-brow' instruments can scratch and make ugly sounds. That's true across the board. But singers ...

There are too many walls?

Yeah. But I'll work on it.

De Staat *is a very loud piece – consistently loud. I was surprised at the rehearsal, actually, how loud it was – you didn't need any amplification. In performance the amplification is used to balance the sound, but you don't need to increase the overall volume ...*

Of course De Volharding was loud already, without amplification. They hated electronics – it was too easy. No bass guitar in my time! Now of course they have one. But yes, amplification is more about having the balance I want. In the case of *La Passione*, for instance, amplification makes it possible for Cristina to sing in a whisper – to make it softer! It's as if her mouth is right by my ear. You know, in the late seventies, pop music was not as loud as it is now. So maybe I am partly guilty for this development in entertainment culture! I was louder than pop music at that time.

What's the intention behind the relentless loudness of De Staat*? What expressive effect does it have?*

Well the *fortissimo* – to use the more classical term – is not separate from the message of the piece: namely, that everybody wants to say the same thing. And what he or she is going to say is very important, and he wants to make sure that you really can hear it. And also that the guys in the back row of the hall must be as impressed by what you have to tell. The other important aspect is that I can't agree with the text, because it's not true – I do regret that it's not true, but it isn't. So I'm also screaming against my own piece. That's the dialectical idea of the piece. If Plato had been right that changes in music would bring changes in society, that would have been amazing for composers, but he's not right ... like the fascists were not right and the Marxists were not right – the vulgar Marxists anyway. At that time it was quite new to think of working with classically trained musicians and PA systems. We – my generation – did a lot of pushing of the use of PA systems.

Obviously De Staat *is an angry piece, and the volume contributes to that sense of frustration and anger. But I think you said somewhere that insistent volume gives a kind of tension to the music – a tautness, if you like.*[10]

It's a way of playing as well. A way of approaching your instrument, which is almost 'cruel'. I learnt this from the jazz musicians too. I was very much impressed during the rehearsals of De Volharding, that the players who really gave their blood, sweat and tears were the jazz players. The classically trained players were giving less because they said 'tomorrow morning at 9.30 I'll be sitting in the Rotterdam Philharmonic and I have to play Mozart'. I was really impressed by the motivation of the jazz musicians – it was more like 'forget the next morning'! Sometimes, the percussion player of Hoketus, Paul Koek, had blood on his hands after a performance of *Hoketus*. He loved the piece. I have a lot of sympathy for this kind of devotion, or commitment.

Can I ask you about audiences? Compared to lots of the Volharding music, De Staat *is a demanding, tough piece – quite a difficult piece to listen to. Does that imply that you were writing for a different audience?*

It's difficult to say. I know that when I wrote the piece I had to do it. And I had the feeling that there were hundreds of people around me who perfectly understood what I was trying to say. And in fact later it proved to be many more than I had imagined. But you cannot count much more than in your own neighbourhood. And I cannot imagine how many people in Reykjavík or wherever are interested. You don't think about it when you are writing. Sure, you think of certain performances. And the atmosphere in this city is very important – Amsterdam's already very different from Rotterdam, certainly in the seventies. In fact, now even more perhaps.[11] As far as Amsterdam is concerned, I was certain that our friends understood very well what I was doing. De Volharding was quite successful – it played at meetings of the Communist Party with 12000 people. So this is the context. With them, accessibility seemed not to be the subject any more. And very similar people watch a science fiction movie with Ligeti accompanying it, and it's perfect music. Nobody complains about it.

I was interested though that the first performance of De Staat *was in the*

---

[10] This is implied by a comment in Andriessen 1968d (p. 181) where he equates varying dynamics, not just with 'strength of sound' but with varying degrees of 'musical tension'.

[11] In the 2002 elections, the extremist politician Pim Fortuyn had particular success in Rotterdam.

Concertgebouw, which I associate with 'high art' culture and a select audience. I suppose the question is: who is your audience?

Well, the Concertgebouw *is* basically for classical and Romantic music. But there were also a few new music concerts; and certainly there were jazz concerts there for years. When I was 15 I saw Miles Davis there, and other people too. So it was not completely forbidden to go to the Concertgebouw: when there were good people playing you went there. However, the fact that we worked in new venues was also very important. Because of the activities of my generation in the sixties and early seventies, there are many more concert halls in Amsterdam. Like Paradiso – that didn't exist before. Felix Meritis didn't exist; Frascati, all kinds of things.[12] But I think this has more to do with what the Germans call the *Zeitgeist*. At that time there was an enormous hunger for new cultural activities – new theatre, happenings, body art, different sorts of performance. So the whole atmosphere helped a lot.

At that time I was very pragmatic: I said that the audience for this kind of performance – I always saw myself together with other musicians, with jazz composers such as Willem Breuker for instance – was the progressive middle class between 25 and 40. Which was then true. Now, I suppose what your audience is depends on the media you use. So when you write an opera for a real opera company in a real opera house as we have now here in Amsterdam, luckily with an amazingly progressive director (Pierre Audi) this is a larger audience. Because there is an enormous audience for opera – it's very hip. In my youth, in the sixties, opera was the squarest thing you could do! So instead you'd write for little theatre groups. In fact, the way in which operas are produced has changed in the last 30 years very much, so now people like Greenaway and Bob Wilson can do what they want to do. As a result you have sold-out houses for ten performances. And that is a much larger audience ... but it is still, I suppose, the progressive middle-class audience between 20 and 50.

But I don't worry too much about it any more. I think other people should think about how to handle it. I don't see it as a problem. I think people should be able to do what they want to do, in a rich luxurious society like ours. I'm the first to admit that we suffer from what I call 'entertainment terrorism'. It's a big disease and a big danger for the development of mankind. That's very

---

[12] Paradiso is a converted church that doubles as a nightclub and concert venue. Frascati is an old tobacco warehouse building now used as a theatre. Felix Meritis is a grand eighteenth-century building which after the Second World War became the headquarters for the Dutch Communist Party, and from 1971 housed the radical Shaffy Theatre.

evident because it's about money, not about culture. But I don't worry too much because I think people are not that bad and they will survive. The children will always do the things the parents don't like.

I hear De Staat *as being a mixture of confrontation, of an almost typically 'modernist' kind – difficult music, challenging, stretching you as a listener – and music that gives a listener a 'good time', which we might see more as a postmodernist trait. I've always thought of* De Staat *as holding those two in a very interesting balance ...*

I'm not sure it's a combination of modernism and postmodernism. I think it's a combination of other things. I suppose if you want to think about the idea of progress, which is of course the subject of the work, then it gets very difficult. The non-musical subject is progressivism – that's very clear – but the use of the musical material is, compared to Boulez, quite different. And that is now called postmodernism. As for the question of modernism, perhaps the main thing is the chromatic quality of the harmony, which is somewhat more chromatic than the melody. And perhaps some of the cruel kind of motives, which you could compare to Varèse. I don't hear any Xenakis or Boulez, for instance! Far away, Berio perhaps. But I very evidently did avoid sweetness and being polite. However, for me it was a large open world which I entered into, which should be as *shining* as possible. Where I got my material I didn't really care too much. As long as it was shiny and fresh and new.

Appendix A

De Staat – The Text

De Staat sets the following extracts from Plato's *Republic* in the original Greek. This translation, included in the Boosey and Hawkes score, is by A. D. Lindsay.

III 397 B 7–C 2 [= bb. 105–57]
'If it be given a musical mode and rhythm in accord with the diction, it may be performed correctly in almost the same mode throughout; that is, since character is so uniform, in one musical mode, and also in a similarly unchanging rhythm?'
'Yes', he said, 'that is certainly the case.'

III 398 D 1–399 A 3 [= bb. 580–667]
'A song is composed of three elements – words, musical mode, and rhythm.'
'Yes', he said, 'that is so.'
'Well, as for the words, will they in any way differ from words that are not to go with music so far as concerns their conformity to those canons of subject and manner which we announced a little while ago?'
'No, they will not.'
'And should not the musical mode and the rhythm accord with the words?'
'Of course.'
'But we said that in our poems we want no weepings and lamentations.'
'No, certainly not.'
'What are the wailful modes? Tell me. You are musical.'
'Mixed Lydian and Hyperlydian, and some other similar ones.'
'Then these we must dismiss, must we not?' I said. 'For even in the training of virtuous women they are useless, much more so in the training of men.'
'Certainly.'
'Then are not drunkenness, effeminacy, and idleness most unseemly in guardians?'
'Surely.'
'Which are the soft and convivial modes?'
'There are Ionian and Lydian modes which are called slack.'

146

'Then, my friend, shall we use those for men who are warriors?'
'By no means', he said. 'You seem to have Dorian and Phrygian left.'

III 399 C 7–E 7 [= bb. 668–724]
'Then', I said, 'we shall not require for our songs and melodies a variety of strings or sudden changes of modulation?'
'I think not', he said.
'Then we shall not maintain the makers of harps and dulcimers, and of all instruments which are many-stringed and many-keyed?'
'I think not', he said.
'Then will you allow flute makers and flute players into the city? Has not the flute more notes than any other instrument, and are not those many-keyed instruments really imitations of the flute?'
'Obviously', he said.
'You have left', I said, 'the lyre and the zither, which will be useful in town, and in the fields the herdsmen may have a pipe.'
'So the argument tells us', he said.
'We are making no innovation', I said, 'when we prefer Apollo and Apollo's instruments to Marsyas and his instruments.'
'No, by Zeus', he said, 'I think we are not.'
'Now, by the dog', I said, 'here have we been purging the city which we said before was too luxurious, and we never noticed it.'
'Well, it was very wise of us', he said.

IV 424 C 3–6 [= bb. 923–50]
'He must beware of changing to a new kind of music, for the change always involves far-reaching danger. Any alteration in the modes of music is always followed by alteration in the most fundamental laws of the state.'

Appendix B

Bar Numbers, Rehearsal Numbers and Compact Disc Timings in *De Staat*

B&H score (1994)	Donemus score (1976)	CD timings
b. 68	[3]	2'09
b. 87	[4]	2'39
b. 105	[5]	3'07
b. 157	7th of [7]	4'51
b. 170	6th of [8]	5'16
b. 201	4 before [10]	6'16
b. 239	[11]	7'31
b. 264	[12]	8'21
b. 275	[13]	8'43
b. 322	[18]	10'14
b. 337	[19]	10'34
b. 349	[20]	10'53
b. 354	6th of [20]	11'03
b. 358	[21]	11'16
b. 383	3 before [22]	12'03
b. 403	6 before [23]	12'41
b. 409	[23]	12'53
b. 442	3 before [24]	13'58
b. 492	[26]	15'33
b. 499	[27]	15'47
b. 503	5th of [27]	15'51
b. 516	7 before [28]	16'20
b. 523	[28]	16'38
b. 534	[29]	16'59
b. 543	10th of [29]	17'14
b. 552	15 before [30]	17'32
b. 559	8 before [30]	17'46
b. 580	[31]	19'19

B&H score (1994)	Donemus score (1976)	CD timings
b. 668	[35]	21'39
b. 688	6 before [36]	22'28
b. 694	[36]	22'46
b. 702	9th of [36]	22'59
b. 725	[37]	23'40
b. 791	[40]	26'55
b. 823	[42]	28'08
b. 835	[43]	28'33
b. 840	6th of [43]	28'43
b. 867	22 before [44]	29'15
b. 873	16 before [44]	29'27
b. 889	[44]	29'50
b. 893	5th of [44]	30'00
b. 923	[45]	31'05
b. 945	6 before [46]	32'25
b. 951	[46]	32'44
b. 986	14th of [47]	34'15

Il Principe – The Text

Main text from Niccolò Machiavelli, *The Prince*, trans. George Bull; interspersed text from Gesualdo, Sixth Book of Madrigals (1615) (reproduced in Donemus LP recording of *Il Principe*, CV 7702). *Il Principe* retains the original Italian.

1. But since my intention is to say something that will prove of practical use to the inquirer, I have thought it proper to represent things as they are in real truth, rather than as they are imagined. Many have dreamed up republics and principalities which have never in truth been known to exist; the gulf between how one should live and how one does live is so wide that a man who neglects what is actually done for what should be done learns the way to self-destruction rather than self-preservation. The fact is that a man who wants to act virtuously in every way necessarily comes to grief among so many who are not virtuous. Therefore if a prince wants to maintain his rule he must learn how not to be virtuous, and to make use of this or not according to need.

   I. Oh, so little sorrow.

2. Indeed, there is no surer way of keeping possession than by devastation. Whoever becomes the master of a city accustomed to freedom, and does not destroy it, may expect to be destroyed himself; because, when there is a rebellion, such a city justifies itself by calling on the name of liberty and its ancient institutions, never forgotten despite the passing of time and the benefits received from the new ruler. Whatever the conqueror's actions or foresight, if the inhabitants are not dispersed and scattered, they will forget neither that name nor those institutions; and at the first opportunity they will at once have recourse to them.

   II. I die, fatigued.

3. It should be borne in mind that there is nothing more difficult to arrange, more doubtful of success, and more dangerous to carry through than initiating changes in a state's constitution. The innovator makes enemies of all those who prospered under the old order, and only lukewarm support is forthcoming from those who would prosper under the new ... never really trusting new things unless they have tested them by experience.

III. It no longer troubles me.

4. That is why all armed prophets have conquered, and unarmed prophets have come to grief.

5. I believe that here it is a question of cruelty used well or badly. We can say that cruelty is used well (if it is permissible to talk in this way of what is evil) when it is employed once for all, and one's safety depends on it, and then it is not persisted in but as far as possible turned to the good of one's subjects.

IV. Cruel thoughts.

6. A man who becomes prince by favour of the people finds himself standing alone, and he has near him either no one or very few not prepared to take orders.... The people are more honest in their intentions than the nobles are, because the latter want to oppress the people, whereas they want only not to be oppressed.

7. From this arises the following question: whether it is better to be loved than feared, or the reverse. The answer is that one would like to be both the one and the other; but because it is difficult to combine them, it is far better to be feared than loved.

V. It no longer troubles me.

8. Because men sooner forget the death of their father than the loss of their patrimony.

9. So let a prince set about the task of conquering and maintaining his state; his methods will always be judged honourable and will be universally praised. The common people are always impressed by appearances and results. In this context, there are only common people, and there is no room for the few when the many are supported by the state.

10. ... that whoever is responsible for another's becoming powerful ruins himself.

11. Men will always do badly by you unless they are forced to be good.

Bibliography

Akkeren, Arnold van (1977), 'Ancient Greek music', *Key Notes*, **6**, 45.

Andriessen, Louis (1963), 'Visit to Darmstadt', in Andriessen 2002, pp. 114–18.

—— (1966), 'Mendelssohn, fizzy drinks and the avant-garde', in Andriessen 2002, pp. 52–56.

—— (1968a), 'Carlo Gesualdo di Venosa', in Andriessen 2002, pp. 87–94.

—— (1968b), 'Guillaume de Machaut and the *Messe de Nostre Dame*', in Andriessen 2002, pp. 80–86.

—— (1968c), 'Muzikale en politieke commentaren en analyses bij een programma van een politiek demonstratief experimenteel concert', in *Programma Politiek-demonstratief experimenteel concert* (Amsterdam: Querido).

—— (1968d), 'De tijd in tegenspraak', *De Gids*, **8**, 178–81.

—— (1972), 'Brief history of De Volharding', in Andriessen 2002, pp. 128–36.

—— (1975), 'Komponeren voor "De Maatregel"', *Te elfder ure*, **22**, 429–46.

—— (1976), 'Letter from a composer to a writer', in Andriessen 2002, pp. 57–59.

—— (1977a), 'About the open strings project', in Andriessen 2002, pp. 139–41.

—— (1977b), notes to *De Staat*, *Il Duce*, *Il Principe* and *Hoketus*, *Key Notes*, **6**, 42–44.

—— (1978), 'Music theatre in the Netherlands', in Boezem and Peters (eds) 1994, pp. 48–50.

—— (1990a), 'Crossing the cultural landscape', in Jetteke Bolten (ed.), *Straight through Culture* (Amsterdam: De Balie), pp. 99–102.

—— (1990b), 'Interview on *De Staat*' with Ruth Dreier, in Andriessen 2002, pp. 148–56.

—— (1995a), 'The forgotten masterpiece', in Andriessen 2002, pp. 71–72.

—— (1995b), 'Reinbert, een tuinstoeltje en de Amerikanse connectie', in Peter Peters (ed.), *Zoeken naar het ongehoorde: Twintig jaar Schönberg Ensemble* (Amsterdam: International Theatre and Film Books), pp. 108–15.

—— (1996a), 'Composer of genius', in Andriessen 2002, pp. 99–108.

—— (1996b), 'Héél hard schreeuwen!', in Elmer Schönberger et al. (eds), *Ssst! Nieuwe ensembles voor nieuwe muziek* (Amsterdam: International Theatre and Film Books), pp. 116–19.

—— (1997/1999a), '*Dancing on the Bones*', in Andriessen 2002, pp. 293–300.

—— (1997/1999b), '*The Last Day*', in Andriessen 2002, pp. 274–82.

—— (1997/1999c), '*Trilogy of the Last Day*', in Andriessen 2002, pp. 267–73.

—— (1998a), 'Romantic irony', in Andriessen 2002, pp. 73–74.

—— (1998b), '*Rosa, a Horse Drama*', in Andriessen 2002, pp. 242–66.

—— (2000), '*Writing to Vermeer*', in Andriessen 2002, pp. 301–32.

—— (2001), '*Trilogie van de Laatste Dag*', *Tijdschrift voor Muziektheorie*, **6** (3), 213–21.

—— (2002), *The Art of Stealing Time*, ed. Mirjam Zegers, trans. Clare Yates (Todmorden, Lancs: Arc).

—— and Jonathan Cross (2003), 'Composing with Stravinsky', in Jonathan Cross (ed.), *The Cambridge Companion to Stravinsky* (Cambridge: Cambridge University Press), pp. 249–57.

—— and Edward Harsh (1992), 'The past as a presence in Part One of Louis Andriessen's *De Materie*', *Contemporary Music Review*, **6** (2), 59–70.

—— and Elmer Schönberger (1979), 'Componeren: een les', *Muziek en Dans*, **3** (1), 13–16.

—— —— (1981), 'On the conceiving of time', *Key Notes*, **13**, 5–11. Reprinted in revised translation in Andriessen 2002, pp. 155–74.

—— —— (1989), *The Apollonian Clockwork: On Stravinsky*, trans. Jeff Hamburg (Oxford: Oxford University Press).

—— and Paulien Terreehorst (1981), 'Wie voltrekt het kunstwerk?', *NRC Handelsblad*, 17 June, p. 12.

—— and Gavin Thomas (1994), 'Life downtown', *Musical Times*, **135** (March), 138–42.

Barker, Andrew (ed.) (1984), *Greek Musical Writings*, i: *The Musician and his Art* (Cambridge: Cambridge University Press).

Beer, Roland de (1981), 'Wie heeft mij gevaarlijk gevonden?', *De Volkskrant*, 9 May, p. 31.

—— (1985), 'The awesome symphony orchestra', *Key Notes*, **21**, 26–32.

—— (1994), 'Tegen de toplaag, tegen de kunstpausen', *De Volkskrant*, 'Kunst en Cultuur' supplement, 11 November, p. 4.

Bernlef, J. (1981), 'Vrijheden en verboden: een gesprek met Louis Andriessen en Misha Mengelberg', *Raster*, **19**, 88–105.

Betz, Albrecht (1982), *Hanns Eisler: Political Musician*, trans. Bill Hopkins (Cambridge: Cambridge University Press).

Björnberg, Alf (1984), 'Aeolian harmony in contemporary popular music', <http://www.theblackbook.net/acad/tagg/others/bjbgeol.html>, accessed 25 March 2003.

Boezem, Maria-Rosa, and Philip Peters (eds) (1994), *Forum 1977–1987: Explorations of Art from Beyond the Fringe* (Eindhoven: Kempen).

Brecht, Bertolt (1964), *Brecht on Theatre: The Development of an Aesthetic*, ed. and trans. John Willett (New York: Hill and Wang).

—— (1997), *Bertolt Brecht: Plays, Poetry and Prose – The Collected Plays: Volume Three Part Two*, ed. John Willett, trans. John Willett et al. (London: Methuen).

Brown, Bernard E. (1974), *Protest in Paris: Anatomy of a Revolt* (Norristown, NJ: General Learning Press).

Brubeck, Darius (2002), '1959: the beginning of beyond', in Cooke and Horn (eds) 2002, pp. 177–201.

Cardew, Cornelius (1974), *Stockhausen Serves Imperialism* (London: Latimer New Dimensions).

Cone, Edward T. (1962), 'Stravinsky: the progress of a method', *Perspectives of New Music*, **1** (1), 18–26.

Cooke, Mervyn (1998), '"The East in the West": evocations of the gamelan in Western music', in Jonathan Bellman (ed.), *The Exotic in Western Music* (Boston: Northeastern University Press), pp. 258–80.

—— and David Horn (eds) (2002), *The Cambridge Companion to Jazz* (Cambridge: Cambridge University Press).

Coul, Ferd op de (1979), 'Andere muziek maken is andere levenshouding', *Nieuwsblad van het Zuiden*, 6 September.

Cross, Jonathan (1998), *The Stravinsky Legacy* (Cambridge: Cambridge University Press).

Desmedt, Els (1988), 'Louis Andriessen: eerste muziek, dan politiek', unpublished Licentiaat Diploma thesis, Rijksuniversiteit Gent.

Eisler, Hanns (1978), *A Rebel in Music: Selected Writings*, ed. Manfred Grabs, trans. Marjorie Meyer (Berlin: Seven Seas Publishers).

Enright, Robert (1996), 'Notes towards anarchy: an interview with Louis Andriessen', *Border Crossings*, **15** (1), 32–38.

Everett, Yayoi Uno (forthcoming), *The Music of Louis Andriessen: Politics, Parody and Crossing Boundaries* (Cambridge: Cambridge University Press).

Ford, Andrew (1993), *Composer to Composer: Conversations about Contemporary Music* (London: Quartet).

Fowler, Bridget (1997), *Pierre Bourdieu and Cultural Theory: Critical Investigations* (London: Sage Publications).

Giskes, Johan, et al. (1991), *Waar bemoei je je mee: 75 jaar belangenstrijd van de Vereniging 'Het Concertgebouworkest'* (Zutphen: Walburg Pers).

Goedegebuure, Jaap, and Anne Marie Musschoot (1991), *Contemporary Fiction of the Low Countries* (Rekkem: Stichting Ons Erfdeel).

Gridley, Mark C. (2000), *Jazz Styles: History and Analysis*, 7th edn (Upper Saddle River, NJ: Prentice Hall).

Grijp, Louis Peter (ed.) (2001), *Een muziekgeschiedenis der Nederlanden* (Amsterdam: Amsterdam University Press).

Gronemeyer, Gisela (1992), 'Spiel nach strengen Regeln: der holländische Komponist Louis Andriessen', *Neue Zeitschrift für Musik*, **153** (7/8), 52–57.

Hartwell, Robin (1993), 'Postmodernism and art music', in Simon Miller (ed.), *The Last Post: Music after Modernism* (Manchester: Manchester University Press), pp. 27–51.

Heile, Björn (2002), 'Collage vs. compositional control: the interdependency of modernist and postmodernist approaches in the work of Mauricio Kagel', in Lochhead and Auner (eds) 2002, pp. 287–99.

Hiu, Pay-Uun (1993), 'De Haagse hik', in Van der Waa (ed.) 1993, pp. 72–87.

Hoekstra, Han (1968), 'Madurodam-revolutie in Carré', *Het Parool*, 1 June.

Hulsman, Bernard (1995), 'Louis Andriessen over Janet Jackson', *NRC Handelsblad*, 20 March, p. 8.

Jackson, Travis A. (2002), 'Jazz as musical practice', in Cooke and Horn (eds) 2002, pp. 83–95.

Jansen, Kasper (1980), 'Bruno Maderna and Dutch concert life', *Key Notes*, **11**, 31–36.

Johnson, Timothy A. (1994), 'Minimalism: aesthetic, style, or technique?', *Musical Quarterly*, **78**, 742–73.

Kellein, Thomas (1995), *Fluxus* (London: Thames and Hudson).

Kellner, Douglas (1997), 'Brecht's Marxist aesthetic', in *Illuminations: The Critical Theory Web Site*, <http://www.uta.edu/huma/illuminations/kell3.htm>, accessed 29 April 2003.

Kennedy, James C. (1995), 'Building New Babylon: Cultural Change in the Netherlands during the 1960s', Ph.D. thesis, University of Iowa; published in translation as *Nieuw Babylon in aanbouw: Nederland in de jaren zestig* (Amsterdam: Boom).

Kernfeld, Barry (1995), *What to Listen for in Jazz* (New Haven: Yale University Press).

Kimberley, Nick (1994), 'Agent of change', *The Wire*, **124** (June), 36–38.

Klis, Jolande van der (ed.) (2000), *The Essential Guide to Dutch Music: 100 Composers and their Work* (Amsterdam: Amsterdam University Press).

Kolsteeg, Johan (1997), *Eén groot oeuvre – Donemus: vijftig jaar tussen componisten en publiek* (Amsterdam: Donemus).

Koning, Renske, and Kasper Jansen (1981), '"Muziek gaat nergens over, muziek is alleen muziek"', *NRC Handelsblad*, 19 May, pp. 13–15.

Koopmans, Rudy (1976a), 'Met gepriegel houd ik mij niet bezig', *De Volkskrant*, 18 September, p. 29.

—— (1976b), 'On music and politics: activism of five Dutch composers', *Key Notes*, **4**, 19–36.

—— (1977), 'Het aktuele muziektheater', *Raster*, **3**, 30–42.

—— (1982), *Tien jaar Volharding* (Amsterdam: Van Gennep).

Krook, Jaane (1976), 'Louis Andriessen: "Veronica ramp voor mensheid"', *Haarlems Dagblad*, 8 May.

Lochhead, Judy, and Joseph Auner (eds) (2002), *Postmodern Music/ Postmodern Thought* (New York: Routledge).

Marissing, Lidy van (1973), 'Met het rooie orkestje van Andriessen de straat op', *De Volkskrant*, 18 September, p. 27.

Meijer, Reinder P. (1971), *Literature of the Low Countries: A Short History of Dutch Literature in the Netherlands and Belgium* (Assen: Van Gorcum).

Mineur, Jacqueline (1989), 'Actie notenkraker: componisten tegen het Concertgebouworkest', unpublished scriptie, Rijksuniversiteit Utrecht.

MINOCW [Ministry of Education, Culture and Society] (1998), 'Cultural Policy in the Netherlands', <http://www.minocw.nl/english_oud/cubeleid_engels/index.htm>, accessed 10 July 2002.

Newton, Gerald (1978), *The Netherlands: An Historical and Cultural Survey, 1795–1977* (London: E. Benn).

Nielsen, Steen K. (1998), 'Dialoger med et værk: analytiske betragtninger over Andriessens *De Stijl*', in Thomas Holme Hansen (ed.), *Festskrift til Finn Mathiassen* (Aarhus: Aarhus Universitet), pp. 279–305.

Nyman, Michael (1999), *Experimental Music: Cage and Beyond*, 2nd edn (Cambridge: Cambridge University Press).

Osmond-Smith, David (1991), *Berio* (Oxford: Oxford University Press).

Otten, Willem Jan (1994), 'The hymn of defeat', *Key Notes*, **29** (2), 14–15.

Peters, Peter (1994), 'Geëmancipeerde arbeiders en dissonanten', *Mens en Melodie*, **49** (November–December), 610–17.

—— (1995) *Eeuwige jeugd: een halve eeuw Stichting Gaudeamus* (Amsterdam: Donemus).

Pickard, John (1994), review of compact disc recordings of *De Stijl*, *De Tijd* etc., *Tempo*, **191** (December), 57–58.

Potter, John (1998), *Vocal Authority: Singing Style and Ideology* (Cambridge: Cambridge University Press).

Potter, Keith (1981), 'The music of Louis Andriessen: dialectical double-Dutch?', *Contact*, **23**, 16–22.

—— (2000), *Four Musical Minimalists* (Cambridge: Cambridge University Press).

Powers, Harold S., and Marc Perlman (2000), 'Mode, §V, 4(i–iid), South-East Asia: Pathet', in *New Grove Dictionary of Music and Musicians*, 2nd edn, ed. Stanley Sadie and John Tyrrell (London: Macmillan), vol. 16, pp. 844–46.

Reich, Steve (2002), *Writings on Music 1965–2000*, ed. Paul Hillier (Oxford: Oxford University Press).

Reichenfeld, J. (1976), 'Zingeren acteurs en vibrerende zangers', *NRC Handelsblad*, 'Cultureel Supplement', 26 November, p. 3.

Restagno, Enzo (ed.) (1996), *Andriessen* (Turin: E.D.F. Edizioni di Torino).

Rossum, Frans van, and Sytze Smit (1994), 'Louis Andriessen: after Chopin and Mendelssohn we landed in a mudbath', *Key Notes*, **28** (1), 8–15.

Royen, H. J. van (1989), *Historie en kroniek van het Concertgebouw en het Concertgebouworkest 1888–1988* (Zutphen: Walburg Pers).

Rupprecht, Philip (1997), 'Line becoming surface: the dynamics of musical texture in Andriessen and Birtwistle', unpublished paper delivered at Society for Music Theory Annual Meeting, Phoenix, Arizona, 31 October.

Samama, Leo (1986), *Seventig jaar Nederlandse muziek 1915–1985* (Amsterdam: Querido).

—— (2001), 'Muziek en het onbehagen in de cultuur in de jaren zestig', in Grijp 2001, pp. 743–48.

Schönberger, Elmer (1975), 'Reinbert de Leeuw', *Key Notes*, **1**, 3–14.

—— (1976), 'From a personal point of view', *Key Notes*, **4**, 36–38.

—— (1993), 'Het Stravinsky-gevoel', in Van der Waa (ed.) 1993, pp. 210–37.

—— (1996), booklet note to compact disc of *Nocturnen* etc. (Donemus Composers' Voice Highlights, CV54).

—— (1998), 'Introduction', brochure on Louis Andriessen (London: Boosey and Hawkes).

—— (2000), 'Andriessen, Louis', in *New Grove Dictionary of Music and Musicians*, 2nd edn, ed. Stanley Sadie and John Tyrrell (London: Macmillan), vol. 1, pp. 637–40.

Schouten, Martin (1973), 'Hoe De Zestigers de Nederlandse muziek uit de droom hielpen', *Haagse Post*, **60** (44), 3 November, 56–66.

—— (1974), 'Louis Andriessen en zijn rode kapel', *Haagse Post*, **61** (30), 27 July, 26–31.

Schwarz, K. Robert (1996), *Minimalists* (London: Phaidon).

Shetter, William Z. (1987), *The Netherlands in Perspective: The Organizations of Society and Environment* (Leiden: Neihoff).

Solomon, Larry (2003), 'The table of pitch-class sets', <http://music.theory.home.att.net/pcsets.htm>, accessed 25 March 2003.

Steenhuis, Aafke, and Barend Wijtman (1976), '"Mensen moeten ophouden met te doen wat meneer zegt": gesprek met Louis Andriessen', *Groene Amsterdammer*, 28 July, pp. 3–4.

Straus, Joseph (1990), *Introduction to Post-Tonal Theory* (Englewood Cliffs, NJ: Prentice Hall).

Stravinsky, Igor (1947), *The Poetics of Music in the Form of Six Lessons*, trans. Arthur Knodel and Ingolf Dahl (Cambridge, Mass.: Harvard University Press).

—— (1962), *An Autobiography* (New York: W. W. Norton).

Strunk, Steven (2002), 'Harmony', in *New Grove Dictionary of Jazz*, 2nd edn, ed. Barry Kernfeld (London: Macmillan), vol. 2, pp. 159–72.

Taruskin, Richard (1996), *Stravinsky and the Russian Traditions: A Biography of the Works Through 'Mavra'*, 2 vols (Oxford: Oxford University Press).

Tra, Gijs (1978), 'De Volharding: "an offbeat jazz group or a crazy band of wind players"', *Key Notes*, **7**, 10–12.

Trochimczyk, Maja (ed.) (2002), *The Music of Louis Andriessen* (New York: Routledge).

Vermeulen, Ernst (1989), 'Notenkrakers schiepen ruimte voor het allernieuwste', *Mens en Melodie*, **44** (5), 297–301.

—— (1992), 'Kees van Baaren's antischool', *Key Notes*, **26** (1), 14–17.

—— (1994), 'Reconstructie van een revolutie', *Entr'acte*, **6** (8), 21–23.

Voeten, Teun (1990), 'Dutch Provos', *High Times*, January, pp. 32–36, 64–66, 73.

Vries, Klaas de (1976), 'Andriessen: *De Staat*', source unknown (stored in Muziekgroep Nederland archive).

Waa, Frits van der (ed.) (1993), *De slag van Andriessen* (Amsterdam: De Bezige Bij).

—— (2000), 'Louis Andriessen', in Van der Klis 2000, pp. 14–18.

Walsh, Stephen (1993), *Stravinsky: Oedipus rex* (Cambridge: Cambridge University Press).

West, M. L. (1992), *Ancient Greek Music* (Oxford: Clarendon Press).

Whitehead, Kevin (1997), 'Once you start, you keep playing till the end: De Volharding at 25', *Key Notes*, **31** (3), 4–7.

—— (1999) *New Dutch Swing* (New York: Billboard Books).

Whittall, Arnold (2001), 'Three for all: Andriessen's recent music', *Musical Times*, **141** (Summer), 9–20.

—— (2003), *Exploring Twentieth-Century Music: Tradition and Innovation* (Cambridge: Cambridge University Press).

Willett, John (1998), *Brecht in Context: Comparative Approaches* (London: Methuen).

Williams, Alastair (1997), *New Music and the Claims of Modernity* (Aldershot: Ashgate Publishing).

Williams, Raymond (1976), *Keywords: A Vocabulary of Culture and Society* (London: Fontana).

Witts, Richard (1978), 'On Misha Mengelberg/on Louis Andriessen', *Musics*, **18** (July), 8–11.

Wright, David (1993), 'Polity, time, speed, substance', *Tempo*, **187** (December), 7–13.

CD Information

De Volharding (1972)
Orkest de Volharding (Arthur ten Bosch, John Floore, Cees Klaver (trumpets); Wouter Hoekstra, Bernard Hunnekink, Willem van Manen (trombones); Willem Breuker, Theo Loevendie, Herman de Wit (saxophones); Louis Andriessen (piano))

Recorded live at an 'Inklusief Konsert', Carré Theatre, Amsterdam, 12 May 1972.

From Composers' Voice KN3.

Il Principe (1974)
Netherlands Vocal Ensemble, Netherlands Chamber Choir, Radio Wind Ensemble; Huub Kerstens (conductor)

Recording realized in cooperation with the broadcasting company (NCRV) and the Netherlands Institute for Sound and Vision.

From Donemus CV7702.

De Staat (1976)
Adinda de Nijs, Roberta Alexander, Lucia Kerstens, Mariante Kweksilber (voices); Reinbert de Leeuw, Maarten Bon (piano); Netherlands Wind Ensemble; Lucas Vis (conductor)

Recorded live, Carré Theatre, Amsterdam, during 1978 Holland Festival. Recording realized in cooperation with the NOS television department.

From Donemus Composers' Voice CV7702/c.

Index